I Cried to Dream Again

I Cried to Dream Again

Trafficking, Murder, and Deliverance
A Memoir

Sara Kruzan
and Cori Thomas

Pantheon Books
New York

All rights reserved. Published in the United States by Pantheon Books,
a division of Penguin Random House LLC, New York, and distributed
in Canada by Penguin Random House Canada Limited, Toronto.

Pantheon Books and colophon are registered trademarks
of Penguin Random House LLC.

Library of Congress Cataloging-in-Publication Data
Names: Kruzan, Sara, [date] author. Thomas, Cori, author.
Title: I cried to dream again: trafficking, murder, and
deliverance: a memoir / Sara Kruzan and Cori Thomas.
Description: First edition. New York: Pantheon Books, 2022
Identifiers: LCCN 2021042731 (print) | LCCN 2021042732 (ebook) |
ISBN 9780593315880 (hardcover) | ISBN 9780593315897 (ebook)
Subjects: LCSH: Kruzan, Sara, [date] Human trafficking
victims—United States—Biography. Abused women—United
States—Biography. Women prisoners—United States—Biography.
Classification: LCC HQ285.K78 K78 2022 (print) |
LCC HQ285.K78 (ebook) | DDC 306.3/620820973 [B]—dc23
LC record available at https://lccn.loc.gov/2021042731
LC ebook record available at https://lccn.loc.gov/2021042732

www.pantheonbooks.com

Jacket image based on a photograph by John Margolies.
Library of Congress, Washington, D.C.
Jacket design by Linda Huang

Printed in the United States of America
First Edition
2 4 6 8 9 7 5 3 1

For Summer Reign-Justice Kruzan,

Zuleika "Zuzu" Angel Diaz,

and

all mothers, their daughters, and their daughters . . .

I Cried to Dream Again

1

GG and I left the movie theater a little after midnight. We found his Jaguar in the parking lot without any trouble. He always parked as close as possible to the entrance of wherever he was going. Plus, you couldn't miss it. Cream-colored with a burgundy leather and wood interior, it was the kind of car that made you feel you'd better sit up straight. People paid attention to that car no matter where we went.

GG expected his women to look put together. Whenever he picked me up, his eyes would first travel from my hair down to my shoes before he let me get into his car. If he didn't give me one of his lectures, I knew I looked okay. Tonight we matched. He was wearing white leather pants, a white-and-maroon leather jacket, and a crisp white shirt unbuttoned almost to his belly button. I was only sixteen years old but tall and thin, five foot seven and 110 pounds. I had on a white halter pantsuit and white ankle boots. He mostly wore gold jewelry: long, fine chains, not heavy bling, but tonight I noticed he wasn't wearing any. He liked to think of himself as a classy guy and always dressed in the latest fashion. His hair usually looked like it had been curled but not brushed out, so it would hold its shape. Today it was styled like Ron O'Neal's in *Super Fly*. His big curls were stiff with product.

He handed me his wallet as he started the car. I set it beside me on the seat. My purse was in my lap. I was holding on to it so tightly that my hands were sweating. I worried that GG might notice, get suspicious, and ask me to open it, and he would see that I was holding it like that because there was a gun inside. I tried to relax my grip and stared out the window, pretending to take in nonexistent sights. Nothing was going on at this hour; most people were home fast asleep. It was a warm night, but the AC was on full blast. I was shaking on the inside from nerves, and on the outside from the cold air.

The movie we watched was *Blue Chips* starring Nick Nolte and Shaquille O'Neal, but I couldn't tell you the plot. At one point, I went to the restroom to call Johnny, my boyfriend, after he paged me. I had forgotten to take my purse and had left it on my seat. When I returned and saw it there, I nearly fainted, but GG was engrossed in the action on the screen. I sat back down and spent the rest of the movie trying desperately to relax. My mind was racing, my heart pounding.

After the movie, GG opened the Jaguar's door. He was so tall that he had to bend and fold his long legs to get into the driver's seat. I was quieter than usual that night, psyching myself up for what I had to do. Usually, GG and I didn't talk much anyway. The only time he really talked to me was when he was preparing me for sex or giving me his pearls of wisdom: "Basically, all men want sex. That's how you please 'em. They'll wine and dine you, and if you give it to them, they'll be happy, and you'll be happy. If a man marries you, he's investing in you. He's gonna buy you flowers. He'll buy you jewelry and perfume. Your job is to look pretty, smell pretty, and remember what you gotta do to make sure he stays satisfied." He'd go on and on, and I'd always listen. I didn't care, or agree with him, but sometimes he would make me repeat it all back to make sure I was paying attention.

As we drove away from the theater, I kept sneaking glances at GG, who was steering the Jaguar with relaxed confidence. He parked abruptly and grabbed his wallet. GG always had a lot of cash on him. He got out of the car, leaving the key in the ignition, and strode calmly toward a liquor store. He didn't ask me to follow, so I didn't. I was thinking, "I hate you," because I knew that if GG was buying liquor, it meant he was planning a lengthy sexual encounter with me. He liked to drink Rémy Martin Cognac and 7UP when he was in the mood for sex.

It was about 1:30 a.m. when we pulled into the nearly empty Dynasty Suites parking lot. GG told me, "Wait here. I'm going to pay for the room."

While he was gone, I checked my pager. I opened my purse and saw the .22 Johnny had handed me earlier. The only time I had ever handled a gun before was when my brother had shown me how to shoot his BB gun when we were kids. This one was smaller and lighter. I will never forget the feel of the metal and the weight of it in my hand.

GG returned and unlocked the trunk, my cue to get out of the car. He pulled out a box, slammed the trunk shut, and said, "I'm gonna use this on you tonight," his voice thick with anticipation. It was a Sunbeam Two Speed Wand Massager, and I knew exactly what that meant.

By now my heart was beating even more furiously than before. GG led me to room 115, the honeymoon suite. He'd taken me to that room before. With every step, my dread increased. I was afraid of what he was going to do, and I was afraid of what I was going to do.

I followed him inside and heard the door click loudly as he closed it behind him. I sat on the couch. Everything was happening in slow motion. He grabbed the remote and pointed it. The TV flickered on. It was a porn channel, and GG raised the volume. A woman was on all fours, doggy style, and a man was straddling her, his penis shoved into her ass.

I tried to appear unfazed, wondering if I could do what Johnny's friend, James Earl, had told me I should. My panic rising, I distracted myself by taking mental snapshots of the room. The honeymoon suite was white and red: red curtains, a white coffee table, a white couch with white pillows, and a big white circular bed, on a little platform, like a throne. There were mirrors above the bed on the ceiling. To the right of the bed was a red-and-white-checkered heart-shaped Jacuzzi tub set on a square base, with more mirrors above and around it. To the left was the bathroom. There were two dressers. The TV was across from the bed, near the door. I noticed that GG and I didn't just match each other, we matched the room, and for a second I wondered if that had any significance.

The woman on the TV began to moan, then scream, as the man gritted his teeth, squeezed his eyes shut, and grunted, continuing to thrust in and out of her forcefully, seemingly with no end in sight. As I sat politely, quietly, bracing myself for the pain GG would inflict, I thought about the way I had been treated by the adults in my life. Adults were responsible for the lack of care and attention, the sexual and emotional abuse, the disrespect, and for the resulting lack of trust I had developed. That night, as I sat wondering whether I had the courage to pull the trigger, I was thinking about the foul refuse that adults, including GG, had piled on me without any regard to its effect.

"Want a drink?" GG asked, as he poured Cognac into a plastic cup. He was not looking for an answer. He knew I rarely drank. I mostly stayed away from weed too. By then, I had learned how to numb myself without booze or drugs.

"This shit has gotta stop," I repeated to myself in my mind.

"This shit has gotta stop." I was thinking of everything and nothing; I was both there and not there.

He took his shirt off and said, "Are you comfortable?" I nodded and tried to smile. I took my shoes off but kept my purse in my lap. He topped off his drink. I knew what was coming. It had happened over and over by now, and every single time, I hated it. GG had a sadistic streak. Once he got going, he kept going. And going. He would use me to his satisfaction, in whatever manner, with or without sex toys. He took the Sunbeam out of the box he had grabbed from the trunk of his car and pointed it teasingly at me.

I sighed and moved from the couch to the bed. I made sure to bring my purse. I watched as he drank and started walking around the room, pacing back and forth, as if to loosen his muscles. This was how he got ready. His attitude was always: I'm powerful, I have money. You're shit without me. I sat on the edge of the bed, thinking, "Here we go again. Here comes the pain." His penis was long and thick. Every time he put it inside me, it hurt badly. I thought about the last four years of sex with him, and with so many other men. I was incapable of having an isolated memory: one incident always blurred into a jumble of others. One horror would become entwined with the rest. Anytime I had sex, in the moments beforehand, a feeling of sick dread would come over me. Sometimes I would think about the time a twenty-three-year-old man named Roosevelt, whom my mom had asked to look out for me, told me that he loved me. I was twelve. We were in a park at night and he was coming all over my face.

That night in the Dynasty honeymoon suite, memories of sex with GG and everybody else, and of my mom's violence toward me, surged in my head. GG had fooled and played me, used me to buy that expensive leather jacket he had hung neatly on the back of a chair. I was full of disappointment at my failure to resist a life that had led me away from my dreams, and now what I was about to do might render them even further from reach. Confusion, fury, sadness, and fear took hold of me.

As GG strutted silently, swilling Cognac, readying himself to assault me, I thought for a moment about whether I should use the gun to kill myself, ridding me of GG's depredations and everything else that was weighing me down. Yet I affirmed my will to live. I wanted that life of possibilities I had imagined for myself when I was a little girl. I wanted to run away with Johnny. We were both sixteen and that felt right, unlike this situation involving a thirty-six-year-old man, who had proven himself to be far from the answer to my prayers.

His pace was quickening. He was almost ready. I knew his smell, and not just his cologne or his sweat. There's a smell that men have when they have an orgasm. It's almost chemical. Each man has his individual odor, but that chemical smell is always there mingled with it. I didn't want to smell it anymore. I just wanted it all to stop.

He walked toward an outlet with the Sunbeam, intending to use it on me. He had an arrogance that always refused to acknowledge my presence in the room. A voice in my head said, "You didn't even ask me permission to do what you intend to do. I don't want you ever to touch me again. I don't want you or anyone else ever to hurt me again." As GG turned and bent down to plug in the device, I pulled the gun out of my purse. I walked up to him. I didn't even aim; just kind of pointed it, turned my head, and closed my eyes. As I felt the gun touch the back of his head, I pulled the trigger once. There was a deafening bang. GG crumpled to the floor. I was in shock. The small splatter of blood was not what I expected; it was hardly even messy. GG's eyes moved a little. Distraught,

I bent over him and whispered, "I'm sorry. I didn't want to do this."

The gun still in my hand, I straightened up, grabbed his wallet and the keys to his car. I ran out of the motel room barefoot and without my purse, which contained my ID. I ran to the Jaguar and got in. I didn't really know how to drive, but I managed to steer it away as best I could to a gas station. That I had shot and more than likely killed GG flashed in my mind like a flame flickering, about to go out.

I was eleven when I first met GG. I realized later that he must have been aware of the chaos that was my life. He had to have studied my patterns because he played me perfectly.

I was walking home after school. I lived with my mother in a small faded white clapboard house at 5297 Thirty-Fourth Street in Rubidoux, California. Rubidoux was not a white-picket-fence kind of place. In the late '80s it was a low-income, gang-infested neighborhood. In the streets, you might hear NWA's "Straight Outta Compton" or "Fuck tha Police" and other gangsta rap coming from boom boxes, open windows, or cars, the bass thumping deeply and loudly. Gangsta rap was very different from the music my mom played at home. She listened to Fleetwood Mac and Creedence Clearwater Revival. I was intrigued by the sounds I heard in the street. Rap music quickened my pulse, forcing me to bop my head to the beat. Mom called it "nigger" music. Rick James and Minnie Riperton were some of the few Black artists she listened to. She tolerated Prince and Michael Jackson, but only when she was in a very good mood.

Some of the young men in the neighborhood were affiliated with the Crips or the Rivas, a Latino gang. They dressed according to whichever gang they had ties to. We were all matter-of-fact about it; it was the culture of the neighborhood. Your parents or friends didn't have to tell you to be careful. It was commonplace to hear gunshots right outside the window and to have to duck now and then. No one could afford to move out of Rubidoux. Most everyone was some version of poor. Many of my classmates had parents addicted to crack. Aside from my friend Shawna Lee, I rarely went to other kids' homes, nor did they come to mine.

It was a neighborhood full of mean stares, glares, and paranoia. Constant rolling of the eyes and sighs seemed to underscore all communication. Everyone was out for themselves, tired, suspicious, and afraid that you might have your eye on what little they had, because you had just as little. I never completely felt that I belonged. It was primarily a Black and Hispanic community and I, with a mother who was clearly white, lived between the white and Black worlds. It felt as though I was always peeking out the back door, never quite sure I was accepted. My heart pumped with fear at the looks the men on the street gave me. They called females "bitches" and "hoes" and, in my case, "little light-skinned redbone with good hair."

I heard the red Mustang purring like a huge lion behind me as I turned onto my block. When it caught up with me, a man leaned out the window and motioned for me to come closer. "Hey, excuse me."

I approached the window and politely and cheerfully replied, "Yes?"

I remember when I met GG by something that happened not long before. On a hot afternoon in Rubidoux, a few of us neighborhood kids had played our version of the TV game show *Double Dare*. We created an obstacle course—placing the biggest tree leaves we could find here and there all the way down to the riverbed at the end of the street. The point was to find and collect these leaves as fast as possible. I was super excited and certain that I would win. At eleven, I was one of the fastest runners in the neighborhood. When it was my turn, I took off, grabbing the leaves, and as I reached for the very last one, which was on a ledge near the top of a dumpster, I went in much too fast and smashed the right side of my head. The next thing I knew, paramedics were trying to bring me to consciousness—I had suffered a concussion. It took me weeks to recover from the dizziness and terrible headaches. My symptoms were just abating when the man pulled up beside me.

"I've been noticing you a lot, and I just want to talk to you. I'm gonna go get some ice cream and go to the park. I would love for you to come and join me. We won't be gone long. Is that okay with you?"

Ice cream! I found his offer irresistible. GG leaned over and opened the passenger door. "What's your name? People call me GG."

"Sara," I said shyly.

The door to the car slammed shut as if it was heavier than it looked. I sank into the passenger seat. The smell inside was fresh and clean; the car's interior suggested a kind of power that I was completely unfamiliar with. GG was wearing a tank top and sweats, his hair pulled into a ponytail, but tight and twisted in the back. He had on black driving gloves cut at the knuckles and fastened with Velcro. The radio was tuned to a station that played old-school R&B slow jams. We drove to the Thrifty Ice Cream shop. My mouth watered as we stood in front of the display.

"Go for three scoops of your favorite flavor."

I was in heaven. Three scoops! I wasted no time declaring "mint chocolate chip and rocky road."

"Give her two scoops of mint and one rocky road," he ordered the bored-looking teenage girl behind the counter.

GG opened his wallet to pay, dipping into a thick wad of bills. I had never seen that much money before.

We drove in the Mustang to a nearby park and headed toward a picnic table near the basketball court. Although I was tall for my age, he was six foot four, so I had to pick up speed as I walked next to him. I was wearing a sleeveless shorts jumpsuit, shiny black fake-patent-leather shoes from Payless, and white socks. Sitting on a bench, I focused now and then on my socks and shoes as I tapped the ground excitedly. I happily ate my ice cream cone and watched GG shoot baskets on the court by himself.

This was before everything that was going to follow in just an hour or so, and before what was going to happen in that motel room five years later. I think in that moment, I was hoping that somehow GG was going to rescue me. I could never have guessed that he was going to make my already messy life even messier, and that by age sixteen my biggest wish would be to be rescued from him and everything he had introduced me to.

After shooting baskets for a while, he took me back to his house—one of his houses. I didn't know then that he had a few, and that I'd be calling them all home one day soon. I had never been in a house like it. It was clean, neat, and decorated with erotic sculptures and Afrocentric artwork: framed paintings of Black men in brightly colored suits dancing with women wearing red lipstick, flowing gowns, and high heels to the music of jazz musicians playing saxophones and smoking cigarettes.

GG turned on some more R&B and excused himself to go shower and change. The smell of his cologne and of his body after shooting hoops lingered in the air. I felt nervous and excited at the same time. I knew something wasn't right. I knew that I shouldn't have gone into this house with a man I didn't know, but at the same time it piqued a curiosity in me. I felt I was acting like a grown-up, somebody my mom's age, who would know how to behave.

My mom always emphasized good manners. She'd smack me hard. "Sit up straight! Don't talk with your mouth full. Don't put your elbows on the table." I was so grateful for the ice cream that I didn't want to seem rude by leaving for no reason.

When GG walked back into the room, he was dressed in tight pants and a dark, satiny long-sleeved shirt that he'd left unbuttoned. He was wearing jewelry. I remember thinking, "This is what a real man is like." He didn't sit down next to me; he remained standing and said, real calm and quiet, "C'mere." I stood, and he gestured that I should move closer to him. He closed his eyes and traced the outline of my figure with his hands. He kept doing that, tracing my body without touching it.

He spoke quietly, almost in a whisper: "Don't be afraid. You can close your eyes if you want to."

He gently pulled the jumpsuit top from my shoulders and peeled the outfit off me. He pulled down my panties. I stood naked before him. Humiliated and embarrassed, I stood motionless, unable to move, feeling as if I could barely breathe. He reached toward the back of my ass, still not touching me, but I could sense him. I could feel his energy. The next thing I knew, he put a hand between my legs and stuck a finger inside me. He started to moan. I felt ashamed that I was wet down there.

He whispered, "You're perfect. You're just what I need."

In those early years, he moved slowly with me. Now it makes me cry to think how gullible I was. GG knew that if he was patient and took his time, he would be able to steal my body and my soul. I was so unaccustomed to being treated with tenderness that I imagined, standing there as he expressed his approval and desire, that GG would save me from the misery of my existence. It was his generosity that seduced me, but it was his gentleness, at first, that captured me.

"Get dressed. I'm gonna take you home," he said that night.

When we got there, he looked into my eyes as he handed me his business card with four different numbers written on the back in addition to the one printed on the front. He said, "If you want a ride or anything, call me. If you don't reach me with one number, try the next ones until you do." I don't remember our saying good-bye. I just nodded, as if in a dream, and walked toward my tiny two-room house. The scratches on the door had never looked deeper, and the screeching it made as I opened it had never sounded louder. I stepped in, smelled the overwhelming odor of cat urine, and held my breath, expecting Mom to come flying at me, as if she had intuited what I had been up to.

That was the day I met GG. That's what happened. He bought me ice cream, did what he did, then dropped me off in front of my house. I heard his car leaving as I went inside to the hell of my mother, her moods, her men, the hitting and screaming.

Inside things were mercifully peaceful. I carefully set my book bag down and began to wash the food-encrusted plates, dirty ashtrays, and glasses in the sink. Mom was in her bedroom calmly reading a romance novel and eating popcorn. Popcorn was her favorite snack. She would make it in her cast-iron skillet, melt the butter on the stove, and pour it over the corn in the sienna-brown ceramic bowl that nobody was permitted to use for anything else. She would rest the bowl on the bed. As she read, without looking up, she would dip one hand into the popcorn, bring a fistful of kernels to her mouth, then lick the butter off her fingers, one by one. To avoid provoking her anger, I didn't even poke my head into her room to say hello. I knew she had heard the creak of the door, so there was no need. Mom was frequently under the influence of one substance or another, but she could be a loner too. Sometimes days would go by when she would not leave her room. Those were the best days.

In another world, I might have told my mom about my encounter with GG. I felt conflicted and disturbed. I had never experienced anything like it before. But at an early age, I knew to keep things to myself. I had mastered not crying. I had grown to believe that I was of the least importance and the lowest priority in the scheme of things. The biggest lesson I had learned was that I could not depend on my mother to look after me. How could she? She could barely look after herself.

That night, I lay on the couch and stared at the business card. It said "Felix Limousine Service." I would later learn that this was GG's legitimate business. He owned three houses, an apartment, and numerous cars, including a Jaguar and a Mercedes, in addition to the Mustang.

I was feeling so many warring emotions. Being wonder struck was paramount. I had never met someone who had a business card. I certainly had never been given one before. I thought GG must be a very important person, more important than anyone I knew. What made the greatest impression on me was that he had decided I was worth paying attention to. I also understood that what had happened between us was wrong. I knew I was in over my head, allowing a grown man to handle me as he had. It was confusing, though. I did not register what he had done as painful. My interactions with my mother had, on the other hand, caused me great physical and emotional hurt. I recognize now the shrewdness of GG's approach. He made sure that the benefits, at least in the beginning, were sufficient to overcome my qualms. Without the ice cream, I would not have gone into his house.

GG slowly and methodically laid the groundwork to ensnare me. Even as he took his time, carefully grooming me for what he had in mind, my mother's violent outbursts at home were escalating.

He waited a week or so after our first encounter to show up again, as my friends and I were walking home from school. He drove by, honked his horn, leaned out the window, and said, "Hey, Sara. You and your friends want to go to the mall?"

I was so naive that it never occurred to me that GG had come looking for me. He drove us all to the mall and took us roller-skating. He treated us to burgers and milkshakes. Then he drove each of us home.

Over the next few weeks, a pattern established itself. He'd arrive just as we were leaving school and take us all some-where. He'd buy us pizza and candy, and little trinkets like charm bracelets or fuzzy key rings, treating us the way a special uncle might. As I noticed the reactions of my friends to GG's attentiveness toward me, I could feel myself holding my head a little higher, my spine a little straighter.

After a few months of innocent group outings with my friends, GG decided it was time to be alone with me again. This time he picked me up in his black Mercedes. Sitting in the passenger seat beside him, catching the eye of people on the sidewalk, made me feel as if I belonged in a car like that. It was as if their admiring and envious stares were directed at me as well as him. He drove with one hand on the steering wheel and held my hand with the other. His hand was enormous compared to mine; my small wrist and fingers disappeared into his. We pulled up outside one of his homes, a big ranch house whose front door was flanked with a pair of white bulldog statues standing guard. Fenced in the backyard were the real beasts: pit bulls that GG fed with raw meat and kept locked up in separate cages. They were trained to fight.

The living room of the house was decorated in GG's trademark dark, masculine colors: olives, grays, and black. There was erotic art depicting Black men and women on the walls. He poured me a 7UP and himself Cognac with 7UP. He led me by the hand to his bedroom and lifted a corner of the rug, entered a combination, and pulled open the heavy door to a safe he kept there. Inside were stacks of hundred-dollar bills. I had never seen anything like it. He took out a leather box and opened it. It was filled with gold and diamond jewelry. I don't remember if I gasped out loud, but I must have silently done so. I had never, and have never since, seen such a display of wealth. GG reached for a stack of photos on a bookshelf and handed it to me. I sifted through images of women dressed in gowns standing next to fancy cars. They were so beautiful, their clothes sparkly and glamorous. Looking at them, I thought, "Wow!" He undressed, and motioned to me to undress too, which I hesitated to do because I felt so awkward, especially after seeing the photos he had just shown me. He began to touch me the same way he had the last time. As if he could read my mind, he whispered that I was as gorgeous as the women in the pictures and he was going to give me some new clothes.

He looked at me, gently stroked me, and this time he put my hand on his penis and guided it. After he came, he muttered, "That was great." I am sure my acquiescence gratified him. And in a perverse way, I was both embarrassed and pleased that he was pleased.

Afterward, he led me into another room that had new clothes with tags attached piled on the floor. Everything was age-inappropriate; all sorts of lingerie, baby-doll dresses, miniskirts, halter jumpsuits, leather jackets with shoulder pads, and tight jeans. He told me to take them into the other room and try them on for him to see. I could feel his eyes as I knelt to pick the pieces up off the floor.

He turned on some R&B, poured himself a drink, and paced back and forth, waiting in the living room, as I changed clothes.

"Don't move!" he'd order, as I came out of his room dressed in a new outfit. He'd stand back for a bit, surveying me like an artist in the act of creation. "Turn around. Look at me this way. Bend over. Let me see what you look like from that angle. Do your hair like this."

Afterward, we made two piles: the clothes I kept and the ones to be returned. I never actually saw him return them. I assume he got someone to do that for him.

I was incredulous at first when GG told me I could be a model, but he insisted: "Baby, you have everything it takes to make it." Back then, all the magazines had Cindy Crawford, Christie Brinkley, and Iman on their covers. Girls my age thought that being a supermodel was one of the greatest professions to aspire to. I dared to believe GG, not because the idea of modeling was so exciting, but because of the money I imagined I could earn.

GG would say, "You're tall, thin, and you have that long hair."

My hair grew down past my shoulders. Over the years, GG and too many other men told me how beautiful it was. I never wear it long anymore. These days, I keep my hair short.

2

Mount Rubidoux, overlooking Riverside County in California, stands more than a thousand feet tall. It takes about an hour and a half to hike up the public trails to the top. At its summit stands a cross that was placed there in 1907 and lights up at night, as if trying to mimic the Corcovado Christ statue that stands with open arms overlooking Rio de Janeiro. In 2012, Americans United for Separation of Church and State threatened the county with a lawsuit, questioning its right to erect religious symbols on public land. The organization demanded that the cross be taken down. The potential suit was resolved at a city council meeting downtown. Several non-profit groups teamed up as an entity, calling themselves Totally Mt. Rubidoux, to fight the removal of the cross, which the city council voted to sell at auction. With donations from local organizations and more than five hundred individuals, Totally Mt. Rubidoux won the cross at auction and voted to leave it on the mountain.

Nowadays, hikers on the trail leading to the cross will see a prominent sign that explains that the cross, the steps, and the areas surrounding the cross are not city property. The cross radiates hope, peace, and blessings over the area. I was incarcerated when the dispute over its fate was raging. I would not have supported its removal. Even though the cross did not protect me, Rubidoux is where I lived when everything happened. Many of its inhabitants remain in dire need of grace.

Recently, after nearly twenty years of imprisonment and seven years of freedom, I drove to Rubidoux to visit Connie Nuñez, my former next-door neighbor. I hoped that seeing her might help to fill in some of the gaps in my memory. Visiting Connie was also an excuse to see the house I had lived in when I first met GG. Connie has lived in that neighborhood a long time. In fact, when she was young, she lived with her single mom in the same house I later moved into with mine. She told me that when she first went there in the '70s, she was the same age I was when I arrived—nine years old. Some years later, she and her mom moved next door to a slightly bigger house that belonged to a woman who owned a few places in the area. Connie has been there ever since.

As I approached the Rubidoux exit on Route 60, I could feel myself tensing up. My hands were gripping the steering wheel with such force that my knuckles were white, my shoulders rigidly hunched. I was tied up in knots. I began to feel as if suffocating; I sensed beads of sweat on my forehead. I was scared. I said to myself, "Sara, you're going to see Connie, a friend. There's no reason to be afraid of anything anymore." I had a strong urge to abandon my mission, but I forged ahead.

I turned onto Thirty-Fourth Street, my anxiety in check, to find that little had changed since the 1990s, save for the DirecTV antennas on most of the roofs. The streets, with their unpaved dirt and grass sidewalks, looked as peculiar as ever. Down the end of one block is the riverbed where all the neighborhood kids used to hang out barefoot until dark. The girls would be whispering and giggling about our crushes, the boys would be teasing the girls, and all of us would be yelling about who had caught the most crawdads. Back then, a little water had been discernible in the Santa Ana River. Now the riverbed was completely dry, a camp for the homeless.

Rubidoux could be mistaken for a poor village in the developing world. The houses are small, simple structures, their colors muted variations of yellow, white, gray, and brown. As I entered the neighborhood, I saw a large gray house built on what used to be an empty lot. I wondered, "Why on earth would anyone who can afford to build a house this size do it here?" It stood out as an anomaly amid the other tiny, dilapidated homes lining the street. As I pulled up to Connie's, I peeked next door. The shock jolted me. The house where I had lived was pretty much the same, but outside, it looked like a garbage dump. Inside had always been a mess, but now it seemed as if the emotional turmoil of my childhood was made manifest in the broken, rusty appliances, knickknacks, toys, rags, clothes, bongs, shoes, rubber snakes, plastic skulls, and no-longer-useful tools strewn all around the yard.

I glanced up the street and saw one of GG's houses. I wasn't ready for that yet. I gathered up my courage, climbed out of the car, and walked up to our old front door. Inside, a dog was barking and someone was coughing. I knocked. The old screen door still shook as if it might fall off its hinges. The voice of a man or woman—I couldn't tell—yelled, "Who is it?"

I swallowed to try to moisten my dry mouth. I answered, in a tone so low and timid I could barely hear myself, "Hi, my name is Sara. I used to live here. May I come inside to look around?" Silence, then a violent coughing fit.

The person spoke: "You're the one who went to prison?"

I was surprised by the tears that shot from my eyes. I hate that this is the first thing many people think of when they think of me. I didn't answer.

He or she coughed again and said, "No, that's not a good idea."

I dried my eyes, walked to Connie's house next door, and knocked.

"Who's there?" she called out.

For the first time in my life, I was afraid she might not open her door to let me in.

"Connie, it's me, Sara Kruzan."

Connie's door flew open. Her four dogs ran out, circled my legs, and began jumping up to greet me. Connie has always had dogs, and these were as friendly as could be. Connie followed them out. She walked with a cane and was wearing a bathrobe. "It's okay, they don't bite. Get down, guys. Don't worry, they won't hurt you."

The outside of Connie's house was almost as cluttered as next door. Inside, the furniture was big, leaving very little room to walk around. I counted three televisions in her living/dining room. But, unlike next door, the energy of her clutter was positive. Connie pulled me into a big hug, which felt like a warm, comfortable blanket enveloping me. I closed my eyes and let myself relax.

She said, "Mija, why didn't you call me to say you were coming? I would have gotten dressed up for you. I'm getting over the flu, that's why I'm wearing this." Connie has always called me "mija": my daughter. She hugged me again, "I am so happy to see you. You look well."

Connie was one of my safety nets when I lived with my mom. She was my mom's friend, but she was mine too. When Mom got into one of her moods and began to beat on me, I'd run to Connie. She would feed me and look after me until things had calmed down enough for me to go back home.

Connie is sixty-six. She stands about five foot four and is very gregarious and warm. Her face is unwrinkled and her hair jet-black from a bottle, but she somehow looks and moves as if she could be a hundred years old. It's something I've noticed in people who have had a hard life. Her husband, Ernie, whom she used to call Neto, died some years ago. Her son, Alex, who is in his forties, lives with her now. I am not sure of her country of origin, but she has always spoken a mixture of English and Spanish.

"Connie, I'm writing a book to try to make sense of my life."

"What? You're writing a book? Don't forget your neighbor!"

We laughed, but then she got serious and looked me in the eye. "Do what you got to do, girl. You got into a jam, right? You got into deep shit. But you got out of the jam. What happened with you I wouldn't want for anyone's daughter. It's good you're writing your book. It might help somebody."

"Connie, I was hoping you might help me remember. Some things are hazy, and all that I do remember is not good."

Connie said, "That's because it wasn't. Your mom, Nikki, was 'my way or the highway.' She had a bad temper. Probably from the *drogas* she used. She didn't seem to care that she had a child growing up, and that the things she was doing could screw up her child. She had her good sides, but then, just like that, she could turn into a bitch. From in here, I heard her screaming and cursing at you, and you screaming back. Sometimes I could hear her hitting you. She could cook, though. Whatever you say about her, your mom was a great cook. She did it with a lot of soul and love. Anything she made and gave me to eat was delicious."

I suddenly remembered the smothered pork chops with onion gravy my mother sometimes made. The gravy was always just the right consistency. My mouth watered as I recalled the smell of the chops cooking and the sizzle as they browned. When she cooked that dish, it was my job to make the whipped potatoes.

I took the task seriously, making sure the potatoes were done and that I added the correct amount of salt, pepper, milk, and butter. Her other specialties included bell peppers and cabbage rolls stuffed with ground beef and rice, baked with tomato sauce. She was a white woman, but she could fix up a mean, delicious soul food dinner of fried chicken, hot-water corn-bread, and collard greens. On a good day, if we had the money and the ingredients, for dessert she would make thick dark and white-chocolate-coated, almond-crusted toffee. I had forgot-ten that my mom was a fabulous cook.

Connie said that when we lived next door, she was worried about me, because she and her own mother had suffered while living in that house too. Sitting in her crowded living room now, I began to wonder if maybe the house next door had bad juju that had predetermined all that I had gone through. But no. Mom and I had lived in Monrovia before moving to Rubi-doux, and Monrovia had hardly been a bed of roses.

My mother, Nicole (Nikki) Kruzan, is the oldest of four sib-lings. I don't know much about her family, except that she was born and lived in Rensselaer, Indiana, until her family moved to La Mirada, California. Mom told me that her father, Lowell Kruzan, was a strict, racist, blue-collar worker who had a job at Standard Oil. She also told me he had sexually abused her, and possibly her sisters also. Her mother, Janice, was a homemaker who had looked the other way. Lowell eventually disowned Mom because she had four babies with four different fathers, two of them Black.

My mom is a thickset, short woman of many contradic-tions. She has reddish-blond hair that she used to wear teased at the roots or in French braids. She is heavy-footed, with thick calves and forearms, but she has the dainty feet of a little girl. She is soft, marshmallow-like, but dangerous and mercurial. In the childhood fantasies in which my absent father was a super-hero, she was a fire-breathing dragon. Her eyes changed color according to her moods. Her short stature belied the enormity of her presence in my life. She was into witchcraft, but in a very arbitrary, haphazard way. None of her spells worked. Her sorcery mostly consisted of screaming and dooming me and my sister to hell for misbehaving. As abusive as she could be to her children, she loved cats—and the occasional dog. In the '80s, in my teens, she found God and became an obsessively devout born-again Christian who still used drugs, drank, and had multiple sex partners.

When people ask me about Mom, I often find myself chang-ing the subject. "Tell me about your mother" is a loaded ques-tion that requires a complicated answer. My dad is a slightly easier subject for me to discuss. In the grand scheme of things, both my parents were disappointments. I've had to face the fact that neither lived up to their responsibility as parents and to understand that none of it was my fault.

My father, Timothy Brown, is the oldest of five children. Dad was, and still is, a tall, chocolate-brown man with a big, beautiful smile and very white teeth. He is from a more "main-stream" family than my mom, so his having turned out to be a crack addict, who can sometimes to this day be found living on the streets, is not what you would expect. Despite this, he has somehow managed to maintain a distinguished appearance. His mother, my grandmother Catherine Elizabeth, was a deeply religious woman who worked as a librarian for the City of San Diego. She was also on the city's board of trustees and, accord-ing to him, a talented amateur pianist and painter. I like to think that I inherited my love of painting from her. His father, my grandfather George Henry Brown, was a naval officer who ran the galley at his station. When he finished his stint in the military, he went to college and earned a degree in sociology.

He lived on the streets of San Diego for two weeks so that he could accurately write his thesis about homelessness—which is ironic in light of the way his son has chosen to live his life. My dad's family was never very warm toward my mom and me. Growing up, I rarely spent time with them, but still I feel more connected to them than to my mother's side.

My dad attended Occidental College on a full academic scholarship. He was also ranked number 3 in the United States and number 8 in the world as a high jumper. Everyone thought he'd end up at the Olympics. In high school, one of his best friends, another high jumper named Arnie Robinson, who was a year ahead of him, believed they would compete together. Arnie competed in the Games and won the gold medal. My dad, however, did not follow through. He dropped out of college after a year. He joined the army and served as a combat medic during the Vietnam War. He served only two years before the war ended, but as a result, he has lifelong VA benefits that have helped him with housing and medical needs. Just as when I was a child, he never stops moving around and is frequently unreachable for long stretches of time.

I can count on one hand the number of times I saw him when I was growing up, and they were far from positive experiences. One visit ended with him shooting up heroin in the bathroom, and me crying outside the door. My mother always said to me, "Your father's smart, but he's an addict." She told me he kidnapped me once when I was very young, and she had to bring a pastor with her to get me back.

As a little girl, all I ever wanted was to have a dad who would be around to help me with homework and pick me up from school. Even though I knew the truth about him, I would spend hours daydreaming about my father. When he disappeared, I would tell myself, "He can't call because he's busy saving someone's life" or "He went to an exotic country with no phone service." In my imagination I was sure that when he got back, he'd have magically turned into the perfect dad. He'd be responsible, and of course, he'd be a millionaire, or at least rich enough to build me a huge house filled with every toy I wanted and lots of flowers and pets.

I've only recently been able to have meaningful conversations with him. He still has a limited capacity to be there for me. He still disappears. He admits that he has not stopped smoking crack and drinking, even after all these years, and sometimes he goes out to pick up women. He remains as removed as ever from my fantasy of him, but I am grateful for the rare moments of connection we share. If nothing else, he is honest.

I caught up with him by phone the other day—getting hold of him sober is an exercise in perseverance. I asked him how he had met my mom. His telling of the story was slightly different from hers. He says he was selling dope at the time and making a delivery to one of her girlfriends, who was having her hair done at the house. My mom was a licensed barber who worked in a shop at a strip mall. She cut men's hair, and she was proud of it. You didn't see too many women with a barber's license in those days, and you still don't. When she did women's hair, she didn't do it professionally. My dad showed up to make the drop and stopped to chat. The friend left. He stayed and chilled with her, both of them were smoking weed, and as he puts it, one thing led to another. These days you'd call it a one-night stand or a friends-with-benefits situation, but this was the late '70s, a time of hippies and free love.

Theirs was not a union with strings attached, though they got together a few more times. During one of their hookups, he says she told him she was studying black magic. He began looking for other places to be because she was scaring him. He wanted no part of her black-magic-woman business. On another occasion, she told him he had gotten her pregnant and she needed two hundred dollars to get an abortion. He managed to scrape the money together and gave it to her. A few days before the appointment, he called to confirm, and she said, "Make sure to be here Wednesday morning to take me to the clinic." On Wednesday she told him, "I can't kill my baby."

"Well, can I get my two hundred dollars back?"

"I spent it."

My father thinks that the only reason she changed her mind was because she had spent the money. My mother claims that she only wanted an abortion because she couldn't provide for yet another child, but her love for me, her unborn baby, was too strong and that was why she backed out. What I take away from these two versions of the same story is that I came awfully close to not being born.

The little I know about my parents suggests that my life is a puzzle with many pieces missing, and to complicate matters, I've spent years trying to forget my past so as to put it all behind me. For a while I wasn't sure I wanted to remember. What I have learned is that you can't simply erase the bad moments from your life. You can ignore them and pretend they didn't exist, but I now know that when you try to deny the facts of your life, they lie dormant until they explode in unforeseen ways and at inopportune moments. I've come to realize that to put hurt behind me, I must first acknowledge it. To exorcise it, I must expose it. I must honestly share the reasons for the shame I have felt about being me. I believe that in doing that, I may find reasons to be proud of myself too.

I was born on January 8, 1978, at Garfield Medical Center in Monterey Park, California. Until I was nine, I lived in Monrovia, which has aged far better than Rubidoux. Our house was directly across the street from Monroe Elementary School, which I attended. I loved going to school, and I loved the neighborhood. There was an old-fashioned convenience store down the block from our house called Babe's. My mom would send me up the street with shopping lists scribbled on notepaper when she had no money. They would keep a handwritten tab in a book. I'd pick up the milk, juice, eggs, potatoes, and her cigarettes and run back down the street. Babe's was run by an old Italian couple. Frank always wore a white shirt buttoned up to the neck, pulled tight over his round belly and tucked into black pants. His wife, Babe, had jet-black hair. She had a witchy look to her, with knotted knuckles and pale skin, but she was the sweetest person in the world. She always snuck candies into my little bag. Frank would scream at Babe, "Don't you be putting nothing in her bag. I'm watching you."

Babe would scream back, "I'm not! I'm not!"

As soon as I got home, I'd reach into the bag to find Lemonheads, bubble gum, or Boston baked bean candies.

After my visit with Connie, I drove to Monrovia to look at the two-bedroom house at 437 West Colorado Avenue where we lived in my early childhood. I didn't tense up as I approached the neighborhood, perhaps because, when I was living there, my mom's abusive behavior had not yet peaked. I got out of the car and walked around the block.

The house still has an orange tree in the backyard and a small, unattached garage. When we lived there, my mom worked at a barbershop up on Foothill Boulevard by the McDonald's, where she sometimes bought us dinner. We were poor and on welfare, but our poverty was not as severe as it would become after we moved to Rubidoux. Monrovia is a cheerful town. Coming back to it, I felt as though I could live there now, despite my memories. The sweet scents of avocado, citrus, and jasmine trees permeate the air. I stood on the sidewalk— a proper sidewalk—in front of our old house and breathed in the aroma of orange blossom.

I was the youngest of my mother's four children. The oldest is my brother Craig. I have another brother named Michael, whom I have never met. My mother gave him up for adoption. My sister and I have speculated that he may have been the result of incest with her father. Mom says she tried to kill herself after she handed him over to the adoption agency. She was committed and briefly hospitalized. Our conjecture has never been confirmed, and we never dared to ask her because, according to her account, "I had Craig and still lived at home. Michael was a married neighbor's child. My family forced me to give him up for financial reasons. End of story."

Craig is thirteen years my senior and, like Michael's, his dad, whom I have never met, was white. What I mostly remember about Craig is that he was handsome. My mom used to say he looked like Tom Selleck. He loved rock 'n' roll and alternative rock, and once he sent me a Barbie dollhouse for Christmas. When he was fourteen, he escaped my mother's abuse and ran away to live with some neighbors down the street, who became his de facto family. He may even have been officially adopted by them, though I'm not sure and don't feel able to ask. I lived in the house with him for only about a year. He did visit us from time to time, but that was it. He does not want to be involved in this telling of my story. Like all of us in the family, he was traumatized by our childhood, but he is generally doing well. He has established a new life in another state and has children and grandchildren. I occasionally speak with him and his wife. He doesn't keep in touch with my mom, and if I mention her, he clams up.

My sister, Mya, is eight years older than I am. Her dad, like mine, was Black. Along with Craig, Mya has spent years trying to recover from the treatment she suffered at home. She also does not want to delve into our traumatic history. What I went through, they also went through to varying degrees.

In those early days, Mya was very much a mother figure to me, and she is probably the reason I am capable of loving. Back then she was the one who made sure I was fed, clothed, got to school on time, and did my homework. My friends Alicia and Ethan lived a few doors down from us with their parents, Vicky and Rick. Ours was a lower-class neighborhood, and like us, a lot of the people on the block were probably also on some form of public assistance, but I would consider most of my friends' parents to have been loving and caring compared to my mom. Sometimes we would play in Alicia and Ethan's sandbox until ten o'clock at night, when Mya would come yelling for me to get ready for bed. I'd throw mud pies at her and say, "I'm not coming in," and she'd walk up to the fence on the other side of the sandbox, stand with her hand on her hip, and say, "If you don't come home right now, I'm going to tell Mom." That always worked.

My mom collected people as odd as the "antiques" she amassed from thrift shops. Our house had barely a surface that wasn't covered with knickknacks and clutter, just a few steps shy of hoarding. The humans my mom hoarded were mostly male, strange-looking, scraggly, rock 'n' roll types. Most had shaggy bangs they needed to have trimmed by Nikki. Others would just hang out drinking and drugging with her. She would invite people over, cook, and laugh a lot. The kitchen was plagued with roaches, but they hardly had any opportunity to come out at night because Mom and her friends were always getting high, playing "Super Freak" at top volume, and dancing in the living room. Despite not caring much for Black music, Mom thought Rick James was as sexy and hot as a man could be, and she loved that song. Sometimes she'd grab me to join in the dancing. I'd tease her, saying, "Mom, you sure can dance, for a big girl," and we'd both crack up.

Someone down on their luck was always staying with us. I'd come home from school to find a cast of bizarre hippies traipsing around the house. There was a man named Winky, who was probably only about twenty-five. He was Black, but his skin glowed with a rusty reddish tinge. He had a very knotted beard and wore white painter's pants covered in rust-colored stains that perfectly matched his complexion. For some reason, he always called me Olive Oyl, as in, "How's it going there, Olive Oyl?" Winky was one of the harmless guests. He moved into our garage, which was not set up to be lived in, but Winky just lived there, doing nothing.

One day, when I was five, my mother went out and asked a friend of hers named Bob to watch me. He was a red-haired, freckled man who hung out at the house a lot. He wasn't dating Mom but was considered a close family friend. We were in my room. I was sitting on my bed in a blue dress with a little collar that my mom had made for me, playing with my Strawberry Shortcake doll. Bob sat next to me and suddenly reached over, stuck his hand under my dress, and fondled me. Shocked, I froze. He stopped and left the house. My mom came home after what felt like forever and found me crying and alone. I said, "Bob touched me."

She looked concerned and said, "What do you mean he touched you?"

I pointed, and said, "He touched me down here."

I don't remember her doing anything about it, but she says she told him never to come back, and I have to believe her because I don't remember ever seeing him again.

Bob was just a "friend" of Mom's, but many of the men who hung out at our place were her lovers. These romances never lasted long, and the men were usually about ten years younger than she was. I sometimes thought of them as playmates of mine rather than my mom's boyfriends.

Mom's wildness was infectious. She was the loud, fun person at the party. I think her weight made her feel uncomfortable sometimes, but she had no problem walking around in her underwear in the house. She often wore stretchy pants, but they'd still be tight, so she'd lie flat and I'd have to help her pull them up.

One story I repeatedly heard her boasting about to whatever boyfriend she was with at the time was that she had once partied with Richard Pryor in the Hollywood Hills. The way she told it, she was invited up there and the two of them snorted cocaine off big bricks. This was one of her proudest achievements. She'd brag about it to these young, greasy men, and they'd look at her with stoned gazes and drawl, "Far out."

One Saturday my mom took me to the outdoor shopping center. It wasn't very big, but it was a bit more elaborate than most strip malls. Nestled among the clothing stores was a movie theater, a little hotel, and a diner called Spires. When we arrived, we saw a big sign announcing a community drawing contest. I asked my mom, "Can I do it, please?"

She said okay and took me to sign up.

The lady sitting at the desk asked me for my name and age. I told her I was five years old, and she entered me in the contest for my category. She handed me a piece of paper, told me it was my canvas, wished me good luck, and let me know I had a week to turn in my drawing.

I was so excited. As soon as we got home, I started working on it. I kept the "canvas" in my room beside my bed so that I could continue with it if I woke up at night. That whole week, everywhere I went, I carried my drawing with me and added to it. I still remember the details: I drew a big brick house with windows and curtains decorated with intricate patterns. Atop the house was a chimney with smoke coming out of it. There were all sorts of flowers in the yard, and right in front of the house was a tree. In the center of the foliage, I drew a hole big enough to fit an owl sitting inside it. We turned my drawing in at the mall. The day came when the mail was delivered with a notice informing me that my drawing had won second place! In addition to the certificate, the envelope contained a big fifty-dollar play-money bill I could use in the shopping center. Best of all was a letter explaining that the reason my drawing had been selected was the care and detail I had put into it. My mom asked me why the owl was in the tree.

I thought about it and said, "He's wise. He's a watcher. He's watching the house at night."

With great ceremony, I said to her, "I am going to take you out on a date."

She had a huge smile on her face.

We planned our date for a week later. First, we went to Spires. I proudly told Mom she could order whatever she wanted. We looked at the menu and chose the most expensive items. Fifty dollars was a lot of money for two people to spend on a diner meal. We both had a salad, steak and baked potato entrée, and dessert—apple pie and ice cream. I felt a big sense of accomplishment pulling out my money to pay. After dinner we went to a movie. I paid for the tickets and bought popcorn, candy, and soda.

There was much sexual exploration among adults in those days. We kids thought nothing of it because it was such a normal part of our life at home. Once I found pornography under my mom's bed. It wasn't hard-core; in fact, some of the pictures were of vegetables that had been photographed to look like sexual organs—harmless, but nothing five- or six-year-old kids should have been looking at. Mom just laughed about it. At night I'd be in one bedroom with my sister and her boyfriend, and we could hear Mom having sex in the room next door.

One day I came home from school, excited because Andre, who was mom's boyfriend at the time, was going to be there. I liked Andre. He was young, like the others, in his late twenties, and he seemed to be one of the nicer guys. Something set him off that day, though, and suddenly he grew wild. He let loose on my mom, beat her bloody, and ruptured one of her eardrums. She lay curled up in a fetal position, battered and crying on the floor, as he tore through the house like a bull on a rampage, going so far as to disassemble Mom's four-poster bed, leaving the pieces strewn all over the floor. I crouched behind a chair in the living room trying to make myself invisible, praying he wouldn't see me. My prayers were answered: he left the house looking as if it had been lifted, shaken, and dropped by a tornado. Despite this, he remained in and out of our lives for the next two years, though he never went off like that again. Here was a rare occasion when I saw my mother vulnerable and afraid, and at the receiving end of the kind of treatment she reserved for her children. The sight of her whimpering in a corner made me hope that she would never touch me with violence again.

One afternoon my mom and I were alone at home. This was a rare occurrence, and it felt special. Now I understand a dichotomy: in Monrovia, I longed for those times when things were quiet and I was alone with my mom. By the time we moved to Rubidoux a few years later, periods of calm became rarer and rarer. In Rubidoux, I would have done anything to have a house full of people who might have protected me, or at least provided cover. On this afternoon, though, Mom made popcorn and was sitting on the couch. I went into her closet and pulled out a hat, gloves, and a boa. I turned "Billie Jean" up as loud as I could and danced my way into the living room. I had memorized all of Michael Jackson's dance moves, and I put on a show. My mom clapped and smiled. I loved seeing her smile.

A few days later, I heard my mom coming my way. She was walking fast and hard from her room to mine, and I knew from the sound of her footsteps that I was in for it. I imagined flames shooting from her eyes, nose, mouth, and ears. I had no idea what I could have done to get her so upset, but without saying a word, she marched into my room and whacked my face with her hand. Wham! She hit me so hard that I fell back and heard a crack in my nose, which promptly spouted blood all over my most prized possession, my Strawberry Shortcake dresser, which she had painted for me as a toddler birthday gift. The blood pooled on the carpet.

Mom began to scream, "Oh my God, what did I do? What did I do?"

She ran to the bathroom, found a washcloth, came back, and used it to stop the flow of blood as I cried and struggled to breathe. The whole time, she was yelling, "I'm sorry! I'm so sorry."

The blood began running down my throat. I felt as if I were drowning. I found the strength to pull away from her and spit the blood out. That was the beginning of my mother's headlong descent into a maelstrom of brutality.

My sister, Mya, who was sixteen, and her high school boyfriend, Mark, were hot and heavy. He used to sleep over at our house. My mom liked him because he sometimes brought over weed and shared it with her. Mya became pregnant. One afternoon—and again, there was never an adequate reason for these episodes—Mom grabbed her, knocked her around, shook her violently, and threw her to the floor, stomped on her, dragged her by the hair across the living room, then went into her bedroom and slammed the door. I tended to Mya as best I could, and when Mark came over later, she left with him for good.

When I was eight, I discovered that I could run, and run fast. We couldn't afford the good shoes other kids had, so I made do with my secondhand tennis shoes. I was running during recess when the school's track coach saw me and asked if I wanted to join the relay team. We had a meet against the junior high. When the baton reached me, I grabbed it. I wanted our team to win so badly that I ran as hard as I could, my feet pounding the pavement. I still remember the feeling of freedom, the whoosh of the air as my body propelled me forward down the track. I didn't know who I was, where I was, or that my mom was a crazy woman; I just knew my feet were moving as if they were not even connected to my body. We won a blue ribbon against the junior high students. Amazed, the coach handed the ribbon to me. For a short time, before we moved from Monrovia, I was a star member of the relay team. The coach always had me run last because, as he put it, no matter how far behind the team had fallen, he knew I'd make up the time. I kept running after we moved to Rubidoux, but by then, instead of running for the team in school, I was running away from home.

About a year or so before we left Monrovia, Mom went to a high school reunion and reconnected with a childhood friend of hers named Mike Kurth, whom she had not seen for twenty years. Mike became a sort of guardian angel to us. To hear him tell it, he'd had a huge crush on Mom back when they were in high school. He said that in those days she was tiny, drop-dead gorgeous, and smart. She had always liked the bad boys, though, so he never stood a chance. Then she let herself go. By the time they met again, she weighed about 225 pounds, though she was only five foot three. I stood eye to eye with her by the time I was eight.

They were just friends, never lovers. Mike had been a surfer in high school and was now a construction worker. He says that when he first came over to our house, he was shocked by how far my mother had fallen. La Mirada, where they had both grown up, was not a rich community, but everyone's parents, including his and hers, worked hard and kept up their houses. It was a decent, working-class neighborhood. He said he never understood how Nikki got herself knocked up four times by four different men and ended up a dirt-poor dope addict who had no business trying to be a parent.

At the reunion, Mom got his number and began calling him when things in the house broke down, which was often. He felt sorry for her and would come over and fix whatever was broken and give her some money to buy food for us kids. For my eighth birthday, Mike showed up with a pink Schwinn bike. It had a white basket up front and pink and white streamers hanging from the handlebars. I loved that bike more than anything. It was new and it was mine. Riding it gave me the same feeling of freedom that running did. My feet, pedaling faster and faster, as if fueled by an engine unconnected to my body, hurtled me forward and left me with no doubt that, if I wanted to, I could fly.

3

In August 1987, we left Monrovia in a hurry. Mom called Mike to say she was worried about the Night Stalker, Richard Ramirez, the notorious serial killer, rapist, and burglar who had terrorized the Los Angeles area. Mom must not have been following the news because Ramirez was caught in 1985. She said she had heard that a young woman had recently been attacked and raped near my school. The truth was that Mom had lost her job, had not paid rent for three months, and we were about to be evicted. She found us a house in Rubidoux that she had heard about from a friend of a friend, and Mike offered to help her pay for it. The rent was around three hundred dollars a month. Her boyfriend at the time, a scrawny young white man named Dave, helped us pack, and Mike pulled up with his flatbed truck to help move us.

I sat between Mike and Mom on the front seat. Our stuff was piled up in the back. Dave followed us on the bus.

As we approached our new neighborhood, I caught sight of the cross on Mount Rubidoux. It felt reassuring until I noticed that the streets we were passing lacked sidewalks. My first thought was "How am I supposed to ride my bike here?" A bunch of kids had gathered in the middle of the road. We had to honk to get them to move. I couldn't figure out what was happening. One boy pitched a small, oddly shaped yellow ball to another, who swung at it with a stick and missed. The ball fell to the street, bounced, and burst. Kids here played baseball with lemons.

We pulled up in front of the house, which looked like a shack that might topple over at any moment. When we yanked it open, the screen door screeched as in a horror movie. I glanced around and saw no room of my own. In a casual voice I hoped would not set her off, I said to Mom, "Where am I going to sleep?"

"With me or in the living room," she replied matter-of-factly.

My heart sank. The house was tiny. The walls, floors, and appliances were old and worn. Even the air smelled tired. When you live with someone with a short fuse like my mom, you become an expert at keeping your facial expression neutral.

There was just a thin piece of wood painted white with a latch on it leading to the bathroom. My dismay at this must have registered because Mike said to me, "Don't worry, I can fix that." He went out to his truck and came back with plywood, from which he put together a makeshift door. The small bathroom had cracked tiles, peeling paint, and black mildew in the grout. Mike built a curtain rod by stringing up white PVC pipes around the standing shower, which made the bathroom look almost normal. The living room and the kitchen were one room.

Because Mom called anything old "antique," our furniture was a collection of mismatched heavy wooden pieces that had been thrown out by neighbors along the way or that she had acquired from thrift stores and friends. The place looked even more cramped with the furniture standing on a burnt-orange shag rug. The curtains were pea green. The couch, which was missing more stuffing than it had, ended up serving as my bed most nights. I'd always been a restless sleeper, but, sleeping on that musty couch cured me of that, oddly preparing me for uncomfortable prison cots. I could feel every rusted coil in the frame as I tried to position myself to sleep, so I learned to stay very still. Despite Mike telling Mom it was a piece of junk, she had insisted he load the faded green couch onto his flatbed. It had been clawed at both ends by our cats, so the material hung down in strips. The only light in the room was a small lamp, which sat on a table next to the couch and cast a spooky orange glow.

In Monrovia, Mom had been an equal opportunity abuser, inflicting her violence on Mya, Craig, when he was there, and me. Now I realized that, in Rubidoux, she would be visiting her wrath on her only remaining child: me. But then, to my surprise, after we first moved there, Mom seemed to have turned over a new leaf. She woke up most mornings and made breakfast for me. Not every day, but parents don't do that all the time in the best of situations, do they? I had no idea. I just knew that it seemed as if she was trying to make things up to me, and that made me happy. It made the dingy dark walls of the house look brighter. For a short while, I think I understood what normal kids must feel like when they wake up to a new day. I had always been one to keep to myself, moving through life trying to be invisible, trying not to feel, holding my breath, repressing my being. During those first few weeks after we moved from Monrovia, I dared, foolishly perhaps, to exhale.

Dave and Mom broke up sometime during the second week we were there. Thankfully, he left behind my beloved pink bike, which he had adopted as his own means of transportation: Picture a scrawny white man on a girl's pink Schwinn bike with streamers on the handlebars that bumped against his knees as he pumped the pedals. He was an embarrassing sight swerving down the street, and I was glad to see him go.

One night, a few days after Dave left, Mom cooked the two

of us spaghetti, meatballs, and mushrooms for dinner. We were sitting and eating. Either the TV was on or there was music in the background, and I thought we were having a good time. I still don't know why it happened, but I do know that I had let down my guard. Sometimes I could be smart-alecky, so I might have said or done something that irritated Mom. For instance, she might simply have said, "Don't smack your lips when you eat." I may have rolled my eyes in response, or sucked my teeth, or chuckled. What I know is that, in a nanosecond, we went from laughing and eating garlic bread with a spaghetti dinner, to her picking up and hurling her plate full of food at my head, missing me but shattering it against the wall. I was stunned. She screamed, "Clean up that mess!" as she left the room. I swallowed my sobs as I tried to wipe the skid mark the mushroom-and-meatball sauce had made sliding down the wall and the puddle of food on the floor. I cried not because I found the incident unusual or painful but because I felt I had been betrayed into thinking that my life could be normal and happy.

This event retriggered the cycle of abuse, now intensified and concentrated in the manner I had been dreading since I had heard that Mya would not be joining us in Rubidoux. Home became a war zone. Every day after school, I took my time walking back to the house, which was only a few blocks away. My pace would slow as I drew near. I was bracing myself because I never knew what to expect. Mom's moods were volatile, one minute good, the next, terrible. I would shake the creaking front door to make sure a cat wasn't hanging off the inside screen. If all was clear, I would ease into the house, pausing to try to gauge Mom's state of mind. I'd tiptoe to the sink to refill the dog's and cats' bowls with water and neatly set them down on the black linoleum kitchen floor before beginning my homework.

I have always loved cats, dogs, and other animals, but in a

house that could not have been more than five hundred square feet, crammed with bulky furniture and odd curios, four cats and a dog were a bit much. Amos was a stray mutt Mom and I had found in a cardboard box at the bus stop and brought home. Moses was a white cat, Dolly, a peach-colored tabby. Blackman was a feisty black cat. Bathsheba I named because I loved the name Sheba. When I found her, she was a scrawny, hungry calico kitten. I wanted to keep her, and I knew my mom would say yes. Sheba was filthy, so getting her into the sink for a bath triggered a wrestling match with a towel. I won, but it wasn't easy. In honor of her spunk, I added Bath to Sheba. Sadly, Bathsheba was hit and killed by a bus a few months later.

Those were our official pets. Stray cats often joined the fold. Mom never met a cat she didn't like, which meant that the stench in that tight space was sometimes unbearable. To this day, the smell of cat urine reminds me of Mom. In prison, I had to throw out the few letters and birthday cards she sent without opening them. The pungency of their distinctive odor embarrassed me when my cellmates complained.

The first time I ran away was because Mom was having sex in her room. I don't remember who was in there with her, just that whatever was going on was loud and sickening. From the foul couch where I was sitting, I threw my shoes at her bedroom door, first one, then the other. This seemed only to excite her and her partner more. I banged on the door and asked them to please be quiet. They kept at it. I shouted, "I'm leaving." Still there was no response.

I put my shoes on and left. I felt the gravel crunch under my feet with each step I took.

"She really doesn't care about me, she really doesn't," I repeated to myself, as I hurried down the street away from her and the house. As a child, I desperately wanted and needed to make my mom proud of me. I tried to be a good girl. I did my chores, cleaned the house, washed the dishes, got up on time, and was diligent about school. I was seeking affection and praise from her. The best she could muster was indifference.

I walked around the corner where my best friend, Shawna Lee Fear, lived.

Shawna Lee was a quirky, mousy girl in my class whose wavy blond hair was in constant disarray unless she pulled it back into a tight ponytail. Everyone had tried their hand at getting Shawna's hair to lie flat, including Mom. It was impossible. I loved hanging out with Shawna Lee. She always made me laugh. When I told her what had happened, she hugged me and offered me a cup of Earl Grey tea. That was something she loved, drinking Earl Grey tea in a china teacup with her pinky sticking out. I don't know where she got that from.

Along with Connie's, Shawna Lee's house served as a refuge whenever I had to get away. Hers was a warm, welcoming family. Her mother worked evenings at the gas station on the corner of Rubidoux and Mission, so she was not usually home when I'd come over, but her sister, Judy, who was three years older than Shawna Lee, hung out with us. Shawna Lee's family was as poor as Mom and me, but even though their last name was Fear, Shawna Lee and Judy did not live in fear every moment of the day, as I did.

That evening I called Mom to tell her where I was. Whenever I ran away, I telephoned to let her know I was safe. I think I kept hoping she would apologize for whatever it was that had caused me to leave and commend me for checking in. That never happened. When she came to Shawna's house that first time to pick me up, she told Judy that I was unmanageable. Judy at first thought Mom was beside herself with worry; Shawna later explained that Mom was beating me up. The next time I was over there, I showed Judy my bruises. She told me I could come by anytime I needed to. Only recently did it occur to me that my mother might have tolerated me for only one reason: she was on welfare and received a check and food stamps for me every month. My existence was a source of income for her.

School provided me with a means to escape the unpleasantness of my life at home. In the fourth grade, students were paired off with an assignment to write a book about any subject we wanted. My classmate Colleen Chapman and I chose as our title All About Drugs and Their Effects. Drugs were a big issue in those days. "Just Say No" posters hung all over the school hallways. Anti-drug commercials played constantly on TV. One showed an egg in a frying pan. The voiceover said, "This is your brain on drugs." Colleen agreed that drugs would be a good subject to tackle. In our neighborhood and in my house, rampant drug use and its effects were evident. It was easy for Colleen and me to draw realistically detailed pictures of needles, and of cocaine lined up on a mirror with little spoons and straws for ingesting it. We wrote about the horrors of addiction—that it could kill you—and about how difficult it was to achieve sobriety once hooked. I also think that, in my ten-year-old mind, I was hoping that my mother and father and others like them might read the book and learn something that could help them, not that I even knew where my father was. Other kids in school were able to write books about less harrowing subjects, such as how to care for pet fish.

Colleen and I were praised at school and received a Young Authors Showcase mention for our efforts, though we didn't win the top prize—that went to our classmates who wrote about fish. I brought my certificate home, excited, proud, and expecting Mom to make a fuss over me. She just gave me a dismissive smile and said, "Great."

I always looked forward to school and beginning new projects. Knowledge afforded me the opportunity to transcend my circumstances. The natural curiosity I possessed as a child, wanting to know as much as possible about whatever caught my fancy, was a way to find out about a world much bigger than Rubidoux. I imagined traveling to different countries and read whatever I could about people with fascinating professions that might one day be within my reach. My particular obsession was the idea of becoming a pediatric surgeon.

I wasn't drawn to soap operas and romances, like other girls my age, but to science journals and magazines such as *National Geographic*. I have always enjoyed putting things together. Building something from scratch excites me: planting seeds and watching them grow; mixing ingredients, baking them, and seeing the result. Watching nothing become something is still a thrill for me, perhaps because it continues to have the power to distract me from the sorrows of life.

Often I would run away because Mom had punched me in the face with the full force of her size, or had knocked me down and dragged me across the floor by my hair, repeatedly banging my head as she did so. On one occasion, though, a boyfriend of hers was the reason I fled. One afternoon, after I had gotten home from school, I stretched out on my mother's bed and fell asleep. I woke to find Bobby passed out beside me, his hand stuck in my pants. I removed his hand, which didn't rouse him, and left the room. As soon as Mom returned, I told her what had happened. When Bobby stumbled from the room, she asked him if what I had said was true.

He replied, "I thought she was you, Nikki," glared at me, and left the house.

Mom turned to me and said, "You must have asked for it, you nigger cunt whore."

I was so shocked by her vitriol, I was unable to speak for a moment. "I didn't. Shouldn't we call the police?"

She hit me upside the head. "No, we shouldn't," she screamed. "We call the cops and they'll arrest him. You know what happens if you have him arrested? He might fuck us up. That's a stupid idea."

Mom kept seeing Bobby, so I made sure to leave the house whenever he came by. I told Mike—who had stopped helping my mother financially because he believed she was buying drugs with the money he gave her—that some of Mom's male friends made me feel unsafe. I didn't go into details, but he seemed to understand, and for my birthday he made me a tiny space of my own on the back porch. He built walls somehow, enclosing and weatherizing the space and, for light, installed a bulb for me to twist on and off. The best thing about this little enclosure was that it had a door with a chain lock.

In addition to Mike—a kind man who genuinely cared about me and Mom—Mr. Butler, my fifth- and sixth-grade home-room teacher, was a positive male figure in my life. Mr. Butler loved us kids and it was a joy to be in his class. He played piano, so there was always music in the room. He was a tall, lanky Black man who wore khakis and glasses with thick lenses. He was the single father of a girl a few years younger than me who attended the same school. Mr. Butler pushed and challenged us. He expected us to work hard, and acknowledged it when we did. He rewarded us with a huge smile, gold stars, and his pride in our work that shone in a way I had never seen before. I knew he was interested in my mind, and that made me want him to be even more proud of me. I began to think of myself in a different way. Previously, if I had to wear the same outfit twice in a week because it was all I had clean, I felt ashamed. In Mr. Butler's class, I never felt embarrassed. He didn't care about superficial things, so I didn't either.

I reconnected with Mike and Mr. Butler after my imprisonment, decades later. Mike had heard about my arrest on the news and sent me a card, which led to occasional letters. I found Mr. Butler on social media after my release. He remembered me and gave me his phone number. When I called, I thought he would bring up the murder and tell me how shocked and disappointed he was in me, but instead he said that he remembered that I had been one of his brightest students. He had expected great things from me then, and still did now. He asked me if I had known back then that he lived in the same neighborhood as I did.

I didn't, and was surprised to hear it.

It was then that I understood how truly special he was. If he lived in my neighborhood, he too was poor and struggled as we did. He had faced the same challenges but hadn't let them get him down or get the better of him. He had tried to inspire us not to feel defeated and to push to be our better selves.

Despite Mr. Butler's encouragement and my steely will to excel at school, as Mom's abuse intensified, I felt myself sinking deeper and deeper into a confounding relationship with GG. My grades took a nosedive, and I started caring less and less about schoolwork. I am frequently asked what I was thinking as GG laid his trap for me. I never know how to answer because I didn't know that was what he was doing. I was eleven, twelve, thirteen. When you're that young, you live in the present because you barely have anything to look back on. You haven't yet learned how to navigate complex situations. You don't know how to plan for the future. I was in a dark place because of my unsettling dealings with GG and Mom. I didn't know how to chart a course through adult territory, and part of me still yearned to be a girl who went to slumber parties in a neighborhood like the ones I saw on TV.

I didn't tell Shawna Lee what was going on with GG; I wouldn't have known how to talk about it, and she didn't ask any questions, even though she had gone on some of our outings. I was clearly—and only now do I understand this—clinically depressed, but I had no safe way of expressing it. Every morning when I woke up and every night as I fell asleep, I was consumed by one thought: "My mom hates me." I believed I was the chief cause of Mom's unhappiness, while still wanting her to love and care for me. I had convinced myself that if I could somehow make her happy, everything would be okay. I did not know that I was not to blame for her anger toward me.

Adrift in despair, my life in chaos, at age eleven, I started cutting myself. I'd scratch up and down my legs, deeper and deeper until the scratches began to bleed. I continued to run away. As much as I wanted Mom to love me, I also wanted no part of her. I wanted to be anywhere but at home. Her venom grew even more poisonous. She sought any excuse to call me a nigger, which cut deeper than any knife. I started pondering killing myself, but I can't say I truly wanted to be dead. I wanted to rest, to take a break from trying to make sense of my misery. By age thirteen, I had tried to commit suicide five times, each attempt more serious than the one before.

One day, not long after meeting GG, I went into the bathroom at home and locked the door. My mother kept a veritable pharmacy in there. I opened a random bottle of pills, tossed a handful into my mouth, and chased them with water, feeling a sense of relief that soon it would all be over and done with. Sad and alone, I began quietly to cry. I hoped Mom would soon come to the bathroom and find me. I sat on the floor, waiting for her to rescue me, or to die. I closed my eyes and imagined her rushing in, hugging me, and saying, "Oh no, honey, don't do this. I love you so much."

I opened my eyes. Nothing. In the other room, I could hear her laughing at whatever she was watching on TV. I swallowed another handful of pills and sat back on the floor. My mind raced through some of my childhood dreams: "How can you become a doctor if you're dead? How long is this going to take? Why isn't she coming in?" Now my head hurt; my eyes burned and felt gritty; my face felt hot, my body weak. I struggled to breathe in and out.

In the other room, I heard my mom finally get up off the bed. I could hear and feel her heavy footsteps moving away from me toward the kitchen. I don't know how long it took, but it seemed like forever before she came looking for me. I was barely conscious when I heard her pounding on the door, then opening it, and yelling, "Sara, what the fuck did you do?"

I passed out and awoke to a flurry of hazy movement around me. White men's faces hovered over me. From what seemed like a distance, I could feel myself being lifted and placed on a hard board and carried. When I next came to consciousness, a thick tube was being pushed up my nose, and I could see black stuff flowing through it into a bag. I fell asleep again, and the first thing I thought when I woke up was "I guess I'm not dead."

This sequence of events happened repeatedly—half-hearted cries for help that my mother was incapable of heeding. Social workers at the hospital would recommend psychotherapy; they would ask me what was wrong, and I would say, "My mother hates me." She would walk into the hospital room, a poor woman but white nonetheless, and for that reason they would accord her grudging respect. She would begin her song and dance about how I was a problem child, and would promise to see to it that I got the help they were advising. Sometimes they would prescribe antidepressant pills, and she would swear that she would administer them. She never kept any of her promises. When we left the hospital, she would knock me upside the head for dragging her there yet again. She would tell me that I needed to get over whatever was eating away at me. She would say that she herself had attempted suicide, so what was the big deal?

A year or so after I met GG, my life spiraled down into even greater dysfunction. One day, after my mom—in yet another fit of rage—hauled off and punched me, I ran away as usual to a friend's house. Her name was Jolina. I had met her not long before at the hospital after one of my suicide attempts. She was there for the same reason. That was our bond. She was probably about sixteen or seventeen.

"You tried to commit suicide?" she asked.

I said, "Yeah."

"Me too. Okay, cool, you wanna hang out?"

That was more or less the extent of our getting to know each other. So this time, when I fled home, I thought I was running away to a kindred spirit. After I got to Jolina's, a friend of hers, also older than me, arrived with her boyfriend. They gave me alcohol to drink, and next thing I knew, they were trying to involve me in a foursome. Taken aback, I called my mom to come and get me because I had no wish to participate.

The vicious cycle: Mom would hit me. I would run. I would call her. She would come get me and hit me again for having run away. I was testing her to see if she cared. And maybe, in all fairness, in her own warped way, she did. She always picked me up.

This time, Mom arrived at Jolina's accompanied by a man from the neighborhood. I knew him as someone who sometimes delivered pizza and drugs to the house. Roosevelt was twenty-three, shorter than me, and had a potbelly. His Barry White–styled hair was so heavily processed that it dripped and left wet spots when he leaned against anything, and he smelled of Jheri curl juice. He drove a banana-yellow car that stood out like a pop of color in a black-and-white photo, and he always wore a Raiders baseball cap and jacket and a big smile on his face.

Mom said, "I'm tired of you running away. Roosevelt's going to be your mentor. He's good people, and he's promised me to keep your ass in line."

Roosevelt started dropping by the house frequently. He'd say, "Hey, wanna come with me to deliver pizzas?"

I'd roll my eyes and say, "No, I don't think so."

Mom would bark, "Yeah, take her ass out there with you."

I had always thought that a mentor is someone who teaches you to do something. At first, I thought that Roosevelt might at least help me with my homework, but I'm not sure he had finished high school himself or could even read. He delivered crack cocaine to my mom and, as far as I could tell, had no further ambitions. It made for a very slack mentor/mentee situation.

Roosevelt, on the other hand, seemed to think that a mentor was a sexual initiator. He introduced me to a more serious level of sex than GG had until then. While GG molested me, then plied me with things he knew I needed, it became commonplace for Roosevelt to pick me up early from school and take me to a motel room so he could have sex with me. Or to get my mom high so he could sneak me out of the house, get me drunk, and take me to the park at night, where he would ask me for blow jobs and slap his penis on my face when he came. At the same time, Roosevelt was friendly and affectionate, and I wish I hadn't been so damaged and starved for attention that

I obliged him. He once gave me a silver herringbone bracelet and told me he loved me.

It was a lot for a twelve-year-old to process.

Content to see me spending time with Roosevelt, Mom stopped beating me for a while. I saw him on and off for about a year. Then he started going with a girl from my school, who got pregnant. We drifted apart.

4

One day, GG swung by in his Jaguar and said we were going to check out some cars. He was interested in buying a Rolls-Royce. I was thirteen. I couldn't drive. I was interested in clothes and dancing to En Vogue. I couldn't have cared less about a Rolls-Royce or any other brand of car, except as a means to get from here to there. As always, R&B slow jams played on the car stereo. GG was in a contemplative mood that afternoon. He drove silently at first. Then, in a mellow, relaxed tone, he said, "My life is a work of fine art. It's an ever-changing painting that I am the artist of. It makes it possible for me to enjoy the finer things in life."

He pulled into a parking space close to the front of the dealership, turned to me, stroked my chin, and looked deep into my eyes. "I know that you want nice things too, Sara. When you have them, people treat you differently. Nice things make life nice! Money makes life nice!"

His gaze was intense; it unnerved me. I wanted to look away but couldn't. I knew something had changed but I didn't know what.

He continued, "It's time for you to show me how much you appreciate me."

My instinctive response, thinking about all the things he had given me so far, was "I don't want to let him down."

He stepped out of the car, paused for a second as if about to say something, but changed his mind. In that second, he is fixed in my memory, like an oil painting. It was the moment when he stopped being my "savior" and revealed to me that his intention had always been to make money off of me. In the painting of him in my mind's eye, the brushstrokes are bold green, royal blue, apple red, imperial purple, lemon yellow. There was never anything weak or pale about GG. He was strong and self-assured, and those are the colors I will forever associate with him.

I attempt to freeze the image so that I can study his expression. I think I am still hoping to discover whether he had any regret about what he was going to ask of me. I want to know if he realized what everlasting trauma his trafficking of me— another human being, and a child, no less—would cause.

I try to pause at the moment when he could have taken it all back. But before I can, the colors start to melt and swirl into an unrecognizable mess, until nothing of his features remains.

He said, "Coming?"

I nodded and got out of the car, running to catch up with him as he strode confidently toward the entrance of the dealership. As I hurried, I felt small in relation to the size of the world. I knew that I didn't have a clue about how to negotiate it, and he did. That was why, that day, two years after meeting him, when he introduced the subject of me working for him, I don't think it occurred to him for a minute that I wouldn't go along with his plan. And he was right.

I've always loved fairy tales. As a child, I would cry with happiness when everything worked out at the end—the young girl, living a pitiful life, suffers until the prince comes along and saves her, then she and the prince live happily ever after. At first, I thought GG was my version of this story. Alas, my fairy tale ending went awry. I was about to be disabused of the idea of GG as my prince; I was about to become aware of him as my grim tormentor.

GG did not walk away from the dealership with a Rolls-Royce the day he told me that I owed him. He left with something far more precious and valuable: my soul. He drove me to a restaurant. I remember neither the place nor the meal, only that afterward, instead of taking me to one of his homes as usual, he took me to a motel room, undressed me, and said, "Relax. I know what I'm doing."

I had never enjoyed being fondled or touched by him, but until that evening at the motel, whatever physical discomfort I had suffered with him paled in comparison to my mom's continuous abuse. The pain I experienced when GG penetrated me that night was excruciating. I felt as if I were being split in two. I was thirteen and he was thirty-three with an unnaturally large penis. I sobbed afterward and told him he had hurt me. He replied, "Nothing comes easy," and kissed me all over my body, as if to soothe me. The sensation of his lips covering my skin is still vividly repulsive to me.

Pain during intercourse with GG never lessened. And remembering the way my body sometimes betrayed me when he made his moves, which in turn seemed to infuse him with more vigor and motivation, still fills me with dismay.

He said it would get better, but it didn't. Yet I allowed it. I allowed it every time because I did not know how not to.

GG put a lot of effort into molding me. He had his sayings:

"In order to be successful, you've gotta be able to cater to all of your client's needs."

"The client and my money are your priority."

"Marriage is just another word for legalized prostitution."

His favorite was "Be a lady in public, and a slut in the bedroom."

If you hear the same phrases time and again, as if on a loop, you might start to believe that they're true. This is the essence of brainwashing. By becoming equal parts special friend, guardian angel, and Henry Higgins to me, GG turned me into his slave.

Of course, while it was happening, I had no idea that was what he was doing. What I knew was that, on a bad day, if my mom slapped me, pulled my hair, or yelled, "Get out of here, you little bitch. You're Satan's spawn, a cunt, a nigger, a whore . . ." if I called one of GG's numbers, he would send a driver to pick me up right away, or he would come and get me himself. After GG raped me that first time, he started feeding me candy bars in an attempt to fatten me up and give me some curves. Every time he'd pick me up for a "practice session," he'd have a selection of candy for me to choose from, and he'd insist I eat it in his presence. Despite his efforts, I remained skinny. He introduced the use of toys, including the one I hated most, the Sunbeam massager. Every time I saw him brandish it, I cringed. When he used it on me, it felt like a power drill was hollowing me out.

As he trained me, GG critiqued my performance as a sports coach might. He would say things like: "Do you think they want to see you make that face when they come? You gotta make them want you." Or "Say that again, and mean it." Or "What are you doing? You gotta be the ultimate. You gotta give them the nastiest, sexiest, wettest, legs-spread experience."

As GG was offering his lessons on technique, I was learning to disconnect from myself. I refined the ability to disappear. By the time GG decided I was ready to join his other women on the street, not only had I become a sex expert, but nobody could make themselves invisible better than me.

As her drug use intensified, Mom became even less responsible. She cared only about tending to her own needs, so I was on my own to do whatever I wanted. I would sneak out of the house or go to school and return whenever. She was fine with seeing me picked up at home and returned many hours or a day later, or a few days later, by GG. I'm not sure what she made of this as his appearances became more frequent. She never asked me anything about him or what I was up to. I wonder about the nature of her own relationship with him. I remember once seeing him hand her some money in our front yard. My stomach turned as I watched her giggle while putting the cash in her pocket.

I still went to school about half the time. My seventh-grade class had a field trip planned to Knott's Berry Farm, an amusement park. The only two people in the class who couldn't afford the trip were me and a friend of mine called Lakeisha. She was a beautiful dark-chocolate girl with the most exquisite white teeth that made her whole face sparkle when she smiled. (I called her Queen Lateefa—emphasis on "teef.") I was disappointed, but when I saw the downtrodden, defeated look in her eyes, at being excluded, I knew I had to do something. I said to her, "We're going to go on this field trip because we deserve to go." The light came back into her eyes. I had a plan.

That day, our first class was a fifteen-minute homeroom check-in, followed by a bathroom break before getting on the bus. I spotted her across the classroom and winked. She winked back. When the class was dismissed, she and I went outside to where the long bus was waiting. The driver stood outside smoking. We waved to him and climbed on. Then we both dropped down and dragged ourselves to the back under the seats on our stomachs, using our elbows. We stayed down until the other kids started boarding. As they approached the back, we waved and whispered, "Hey." They seemed to understand and went into action, hiding and shielding us. We could feel their support, wanting it all to work out. Everything was fine until we arrived. We stood up and got in line to disembark. We hadn't counted on the chaperones, holding a list of names. Lakeisha's and mine were not on the list. We were sent back to school, where we were in trouble. I felt sad for Lakeisha. I had wanted her to have fun so badly.

One day, about two months after my training with GG had begun, I got into his car when he arrived to collect me, and he said, "From the moment I saw you, I have been waiting for this day when I can collect on my investment." He drove me to a house of his I had never been to. From the outside, most of GG's properties were nondescript, smallish ranch-style houses. Inside, they were all decorated in a lifeless, showroom style and furnished in dark, muted colors. They were all kept neat and clean. The only thing that stood out about this particular house, and barely so in the dim lighting, was that there was more erotic artwork on the walls, and it was full of people.

When GG walked in the front door with me that day, nobody looked up to see who he was bringing into their midst. It didn't take long for me to catch their apathy, which was as contagious as a virus. If you were polishing your toenails and someone walked in, you didn't look up. You didn't care. In fact, the act of putting color on your nails itself brought no joy. There was very little that brought joy in those rooms. One of GG's limousine drivers was lounging on the tan couch talking to a heavyset Black woman everyone called Big Mama, though there was nothing cuddly or maternal about her. The driver looked up at me and said, "What's up, little lady? What's your name?"

"Sara," I answered shyly.

GG pointed to a barstool. I sat and tried to make myself and my thoughts disappear.

Big Mama's skin was the color of bronzed clay. She wore her hair styled naturally. Her body was round. She wasn't obese, but she had a lot of meat on her bones, and was large busted like the other women I met in the house. I found out during my trial that Big Mama, whose real name was Jane Marie Bob, was only thirty-eight years old. She seemed much older. I also learned that she herself had been a prostitute in the past, but not for GG.

Big Mama oversaw GG's women and houses and made sure everything ran smoothly. Some of the women who worked for him had children. Big Mama helped with watching the kids while their moms were out on the streets. She was smart, quick-thinking, and criminal minded. She had been exposed to so much over the years that nothing got past her. It was as if she had the ability to scan the entire house without moving. God forbid you left a towel on the floor in the bathroom and three other women had showered after you. She found you and told you not to ever leave your towel on the floor again. I never could understand, with ten of us using the bathroom, how she knew exactly who had done what. Instead of yelling at us, she was all about quiet intimidation. Whatever she felt about what we did, she kept to herself. Her energy seemed to emit a dark, low vibration, as though she always wanted us to feel her power. She didn't have to make any effort. I was scared of her. I knew she would do anything for GG. And I knew that if you got on her wrong side, she would make sure you suffered for it.

GG's women were mostly white, blond, blue-eyed, and pretty. They came in all sizes and ages, but at thirteen, I was by far the youngest of the group. The women were well-mannered. No one was loud. They knew not to talk back or question anything. They knew their business, and how to handle their business. That was it. They weren't allowed to use drugs, and GG said he would punish anyone who did. He also explained that, by working, we were paying him back for his protection, his giving us a place to stay, clothes, and food.

We all had to call him "Daddy." Some of the women had been with him for quite a while. We had all been abused at some point and were all lost girls or women when he found us. That's how he was able to manipulate us with promises of hope and opportunity. After I was taught the ropes, I mostly kept to myself, not because the others were unfriendly but because, like me, they didn't want to discuss the trade. And aside from that, what else did we have to talk about?

One thing that distinguished me from the others was that GG didn't require that I sleep in the house. He was, of course, mindful that I was a minor. He made money off of me, but he couldn't hold me captive. I wish I had understood at the time that he was putting himself at risk; I might have felt stronger knowing that he was afraid of something. But then again, he had built up a dependency in me, offering me refuge from my mother and telling me that I was his most prized possession, that I was special. He allowed me to come and go. The way it worked was that I would be at my mom's, and when things became impossible there, I would go to GG's. It never occurred to me that, in the back and forth, I wasn't so much trying to run away from my mother, or GG, but from myself.

On my first day of "work," GG said we would be going to Hollywood. Working hours were 6 p.m. to 6 a.m., and he in-

structed the women to find me something to wear. He repeated "Daddy's Rules" to me:

No kissing any Johns on the mouth. Strictly sex.
No talking trash about him. To anyone.
No straying from where the other women are working.
Do your job as quickly as possible to maximize your
    time.
Do whatever the John asks.
Sex with no condom costs extra.
Be beautiful. Smell beautiful. Be of service.
Do not make eye contact with another Black man. If
    you do, you won't be able to back out of having sex
    with him. He might be another pimp.
At all times act as if this is the best sex you have ever had
    in your entire life.

In one of the bedrooms was a big closet stuffed with typi-
cal prostitute garb: off-the-shoulder tops, short skirts or shorts,
high-heeled shoes in all sizes. One woman, a perky, blue-eyed
blonde named Diamond, explained to me that it was always
best to wear something you could easily slip on and off. That
first night, I chose a tight miniskirt and halter top that I thought
were cute.

As we dressed, I committed the price list to memory:

Sex in the car:	$20–$50
Extra charge for motel sex:	$20
Blow job:	$25
Sex without a condom:	$80–$100
Anal sex:	$75

Weird shit: Price to be calculated depending on how nasty
or dangerous (check with GG)

When we were all ready and made up, Diamond pulled me aside and said, "Before I forget, let me show you something." She explained that she and the others had mastered a system to prevent being robbed. They showed me how to roll money up, wrap it in a condom, squat, and stick it inside their vagina.

One of them said, "You've got shelves up there."

The idea was to store the money throughout the night but keep adding to your package. When it was full, you started a new package and found a new shelf. It was very nice of them to be looking out for me and I appreciated it. I thanked them, although I was never able to get up the nerve to follow their guidance.

The last part of our preparation was getting Daddy's approval. We formed a line and paraded in front of GG, who sat on the couch sipping a drink. His eyes studied me longer than the others. He nodded his approval.

"You're going to be shadowing Diamond. Stick close to her and see how she handles herself," he said to me.

Five-thirty p.m. came, and we left for Hollywood. The night was frigid. In my short skirt and sleeveless top, I was not dressed nearly warmly enough. As I stood outside shivering, I noticed that GG didn't wait on the street with us. He stayed in a car close by, watching.

I took note as Diamond and the others struck a pose on the sidewalk as cars cruised by. One stopped. The man inside beckoned to her through the window. She approached, and he pointed at me. She looked back at me and shook her head no.

I heaved a sigh of relief.

She got into the car, and it seemed as if, within a few minutes, she was already done. She came back like nothing had happened, reached for the can of Coke she had given me to hold, took a swig, and posed next to me on the sidewalk.

Another car drew up and the window was rolled down. Diamond leaned in to speak with the John. I was worried when I saw her get into the back seat, close the door, and drive off in the car. It didn't go far, though, pulling into a parking space at the motel across the street. The doors opened. Diamond and the John got out and walked right into the motel room in front of the car. I stared anxiously at the door, counting time. Sure enough, fifteen minutes later on the dot, they came out. The John drove Diamond back. I handed her the Coke can.

She said to me, "If anyone wants to go to a motel room with you, tell them it's twenty dollars extra. Take them to that room over there, number five. Daddy's paid for it. Leave the door unlocked while you're inside, and when you leave, just pull it shut behind you." She went back to strolling on the sidewalk, street side.

That's when GG got out of his car, walked over, and told me it was time to start. I swallowed the terror rising in my throat like bile. I calmed myself by imagining that this would be no different from what I had already been doing with Roosevelt and GG. And so I just went for it. The best way to get through the indignity was not to think about it.

In quick succession, I serviced five men—blow jobs, hand jobs, quick sex.

The sixth John, a white middle-aged man dressed in a business suit, pulled up in his car. He asked me very politely if there was a room we could go to. I said, "Yes, but it's twenty dollars extra." He handed me the money.

In the motel room across the street, he removed his jacket, folded it neatly, and placed it on the bed. He asked me to please sit on the bed. He didn't tell me to remove my clothes. He pulled down his pants and very seriously said, "I want you to spank me and tell me I am a naughty piece of poopie."

I couldn't believe my ears.

He bent over. I smacked him and said, "You are a naughty piece of poopie."

He said, "I'm a what, Mommy?"

I smacked him on his behind with my bare hand and said, "You are a naughty poopie! A very, very naughty poopie!" I even affected a British accent, which was especially well received. How as a thirteen-year-old I managed all of this without laughing amazes me now. It must have been terror.

When he returned me to my spot next to Diamond, GG came by and told us that business seemed to be dying down here, so he was taking us to Orange County. He and some of his limo drivers drove us there. I was glad for the short-lived warmth of the car.

Once we got to Harbor Boulevard, it was more of the same—one man after another would drive up, point at one of us, and off we'd go to service them. By sunrise, I had provided eleven men with one form or another of sex. The bitter cold of that night, and the realization that I had begun working for GG and there would be many more such nights, chilled me to the bone. "There has to be some point to this," I thought. GG had spent much time insisting that this line of work could lead to something desirable; we had been invited to aspire to the lifestyle he flaunted. I saw women I thought were glamorous, doing what I had now been enlisted to do. I couldn't imagine that they were doing it for next to nothing. Soon enough, I would come to learn the hard truth: we had all been robbed of our humanity and were mere objects of exploitation.

There were Johns of every stripe, but in the eyes of certain men, I saw shadowy evil and had to brace myself. One handed me his money without argument and proceeded to have rough sex with me in his car while muttering filth. He then demanded, "Give me my money back."

I said, "No."

He locked the windows and doors, grabbed a Taser, and aimed it at me—he may have been an off-duty cop. He had a maniacal look. I began screaming for help, banging on the car window. GG noticed and headed over. The John saw him coming and unlocked the doors. I jumped out and ran, and the guy took off.

On another occasion I was picked up by a clean, safe-looking Hispanic man. He wanted us to go to his place, but I told him we couldn't do that. He said it was close by. For whatever reason, I trusted him and said, "Okay." He drove to a house with a well-tended yard. I followed him inside and immediately felt his hands on my waist forcefully pushing me into a room. The door shut behind us, and he locked it in what felt like slow motion.

"Take your clothes off," he growled.

I was terrified and regretted leaving GG's protection. "Okay."

"Stand over there and spread your legs." He reached for a Polaroid camera.

The flash blinded me for a second.

He said, "Pose for me, you little slut."

Hot tears sprang to my eyes, but I repressed them. I knew instinctively that any sign of vulnerability or weakness would put me in greater danger.

The picture-taking went on for a while. As always, my mind floated away.

"Thank you, slutty cunt. Get dressed so I can get you out of here. By the way, good job."

His semen was puddled on the floor. I hurriedly dressed and pulled on my boots. He threw twenty dollars at me. It fell to the floor. As I picked it up, I saw hundreds of Polaroid photos stuck to the wall.

Some men just wanted to talk, which offered me a merciful

reprieve from physical abuse. Some needed to confess all manner of transgressions. Others, absurdly, sought marriage counseling from me—thirteen, fourteen, fifteen years old.

The range of clients was broad. Some I found to be particularly unattractive, suffering from low self-esteem. Others were
clearly well-off or very good-looking. I could not understand
why they felt the need to buy sex. Whatever their type, they
came in droves. There was a never-ending supply of Johns.

At our Hollywood location, some Johns called ahead. One
of GG's drivers, or one of the women who worked for him, was
always on duty at the phone in a motel room close to where
GG was parked. When it rang, it was usually someone with a
special request. The caller would specify the kind of woman he
wanted, and GG would try to accommodate him. It was also
not unusual for GG to take one of us to someone's home. He
provided door-to-door service, if the price was right.

I always wondered if GG might have planned what happened
some months after I started working for him as a way to break
me all the way down. June 21, 1992, was a Sunday. I had had a
fight with my mom the evening before, so I spent the night at
Shawna Lee's—and in a pique decided for once not to call her.
It was a hot afternoon, about three o'clock, and I was on my
way back home. I was planning to stop at the grocery store. I
cut through the elementary school yard, and as I approached
the corner of the building, three Crips gang members, all of
whom I recognized, appeared. One was a classmate's uncle. He
grabbed me. Another tried to kiss me. I pushed him away. He
threw me down onto the hard concrete school steps behind the
building. The three men stood over me. I told them to leave
me alone. Two pulled my pants, T-shirt, bra, and panties off as
I kicked and screamed. The sun had been beating down on the
concrete burning against my skin. They forced me to kneel.

Two held me as the other jammed his penis into my mouth, pulling my hair back to control his thrusts. Mercifully, he came quickly. A second took over and did the same, lasting a little longer, while the third guy rubbed his swollen penis against my face and ears until he came all over me.

I did my best to vanish as the men had their way with me. I was and I wasn't there: far away, in my imagination, I was a ballerina, executing perfect pirouettes and pliés across a big stage.

One of them pushed me down onto the hard ground. Another forced himself on top of me and into me. The other two were laughing, deciding where they would go to eat afterward. When they were all done, the men flung my clothes at me and left. There was no one else around behind the school; it was summer break, after all.

I dressed myself as best I could and limped to my friend Teresa's house, which was between the school and home. I was bruised and crying, and I told her what had happened. Teresa was a friend, though not my closest. She was quiet and always kind to me. We sat in her bedroom until I calmed down. Teresa found a few dollars lying around her room and ran out for Kentucky Fried Chicken and malt liquor. Ironically, we sat on a bench in the front of the school, maybe twenty feet from the corner where I had been raped, and ate and drank.

After about an hour, the forty-ounce bottle of Olde English was empty, but it had not abated the horror of the gang rape. I was consumed with a hot anger. I furiously sobbed and wailed in a way that frightened Teresa. She kept telling me that I would be okay, but I was not so sure.

A week later, I sat on the floor of Mom's bedroom and considered my surroundings. My mom was sitting on the bed, her head stuck in a romance novel. I looked at the faded walls and worn furnishings and thought, "What's the point?"

I went into the bathroom, locked the door, and pressed a blade hard against my left wrist. I sliced the skin open. It burned as though my wrist had been scorched. I opened my eyes and saw blood beading on the inside of my forearm. I lay down. And waited. And waited, until I woke up at the hospital. Bright lights shone overhead; my wrist was bandaged and throbbing.

I was committed to a psychiatric ward for a week. Not until then did I reveal to hospital staff that I had been raped. Police were called, and they interviewed Mom and me. She discouraged an investigation, even though I had identified the rapists from a photo lineup. Mom told the police that she was afraid of retaliation from the three well-known gang members, and that she was planning on moving us out of town soon anyway, so there was no need to take any further action. She also told them I had serious emotional issues and needed heavy counseling, implying that what I had recounted might not be true or was in part my fault. The police chose to believe me but explained that mine was a hard case to prove because it would be my word against my rapists'. I quietly accepted their argument and my mother's that this was a pointless battle to fight.

I went back to GG. We girls and women all felt tied to him by an invisible chain. While working, no matter where we went or what we did, we knew he was watching. Even when I would briefly run off to try living again with Mom or was out in the streets with friends, I knew GG had his eyes on me. We strictly complied with his rule: no talking about him or what we did for him, ever. None of us dared to incur his wrath. He was our boss, even though he called us his "women" or his "wives." He took all the money we earned, and what he gave back to us was arbitrary. Prostitutes are sometimes called "working girls," but "enslaved women" is far more accurate. We received no salary. Now and then GG would hand out a couple of twenty-dollar bills to each of us, while reminding us that he was our great provider of food, clothing, and, yes, a home. On rare occasions, if he was really pleased, he might toss a hundred-dollar bill at one of us and say, "Good work!"

At GG's house, I spent my time sleeping or daydreaming. I tried to keep to myself because I didn't want to know anything. I didn't want to cause any trouble. If you disobeyed GG, he would get very angry.

One day, a woman broke one of his rules. He made her get into the pool naked and beat her with a rope. Apparently, this form of brutality causes maximum pain but minimal bruising. Another time, he viciously kicked a woman because he'd heard that she had said something negative about him. She fell to the ground and curled into a ball to try to protect herself. As he kicked her, he shouted, "Get yourself a hip replacement!"

Every now and then, I would miss my classmates and drag myself to school, managing fleetingly to feel like a regular teenager. After classes, a few friends and I would meet up and hang out. I was required to check in with GG every day so he would know if he should expect me. One afternoon, I was with some friends and didn't call him. Those were the days of public pay phones. Sometimes, you couldn't find one that worked. Other times, you didn't have the right coins on you. Whatever my excuse, that day, GG was scarily angry at me and made me work extra hard and fast the next night to make up for my lapse. As further punishment, he dropped me off on a random street, after I had given him the money I'd made. I had to figure out my own way home. I walked for about forty-five minutes, first in high heels, then barefoot.

The women in GG's house seemed put together, attractive, and confident to me at first. But as I became accustomed to seeing them "off duty," without their makeup and eye-catching clothes, I realized that they were just as tired and beaten down as I felt. Each one of us trafficked girls and women shared the horror of not being able to breathe. That is what it's like to have a man pull your head back and hold your hair tight so that you can't move as they thrust their penis all the way down your throat. Sometimes when I think about those days of being trafficked, I begin to weep. I weep not only for myself but for the helplessness so many others like me experience.

On April 10, 1993, GG went out of town, which meant I had the weekend off. This was great news. I was staying at one of his homes, a one-bedroom apartment decorated man-cave style, with a comfy black leather couch, cable TV, and a fridge stocked with soda. It felt like a vacation from both my mom and GG, so I called Shawna Lee and asked her to come and stay with me. Shawna Lee kept me giggling. She had a funny way of fixing on you with her close-set eyes, creating the impression that she was looking through you, instead of at you. Whenever she was around me, I felt happier, as if I could pretend for a few days that I was just a normal fifteen-year-old. We hatched a plan to party. Shawna Lee had a huge crush on Ernie, who was my sister Mya's seventeen-year-old half brother. Ernie was like a brother to me too. He lived in Perris, not far from Rubidoux.

I called Ernie and asked if he wanted to come over. He said yes, but he would need a ride, so we called our friend Seth, who had a reputation for always knowing how to get hold of a car, whether borrowed from a friend, his family, or gotten by other means. Seth's dad was a pastor, but Seth, who was only fourteen, was decidedly not following in his father's godly footsteps. He showed up driving a Jeep Cherokee. We didn't know it was stolen until we got inside and he told us he had jacked it.

I was in the passenger seat. We picked up Ernie, who sat

in the back with Shawna Lee. Ernie and Seth wanted to stop at Walmart to get snacks for our party. As we headed there, Seth proposed as a lark that I get behind the steering wheel. It would be fun, he thought, to see me drive. Beyond stepping on the gas and the brakes, I didn't know how.

The steering was hard to control, probably because Seth had jammed a screwdriver into the ignition to start the car. My driving was all over the place. I was zigzagging across lanes like someone who had had way too much to drink. My three passengers laughed their heads off all the way to Walmart, where I parked crookedly. Ernie and Seth said they would be back in ten minutes and went inside.

Shawna Lee and I listened to music and joked around as we waited in the car. I teased her about the fact that Ernie was eyeing her with definite romantic interest. It was a moment of pure teenage euphoria, and I relished it for its rarity. Ten minutes later, Ernie and Seth came running out of the store with armfuls of merchandise they'd lifted.

"Go! Go! Go!" they yelled as they jumped into the car.

I stepped on the gas and got us out of there. A few blocks later I merged onto the freeway, but Seth told me to pull off at the next exit so he could get back in the driver's seat.

After he had been driving for a little while, we noticed a police car tailing us and signaling for us to pull over. The officer got out of the sedan, walked up, and told us he was stopping us for failing to signal a turn farther back. He poked his head into the car window and noticed the screwdriver and wires sticking out of the ignition. His eyes narrowed as he asked Seth for his license and registration.

Mary J. Blige's "What's the 411?" was blaring on the car stereo, and my heart was pounding as Seth cheerfully said, "Hold on" to the officer.

Seth reached past me to pretend he was going to get the

registration and license out of the glove compartment, but I could tell by his expression that he was getting ready to ditch this cop.

Seth looked back at the cop, smiled, flipped his middle finger, and stepped on the gas. As if in a movie, we pulled away at top speed, red and blue lights flashing and sirens blaring in our wake. Soon we heard the hum of the Riverside Police helicopter flying overhead. It trained a spotlight on us, and a disembodied voice bellowed over the loudspeaker.

"This is the LAPD. Pull over immediately!"

Seth ignored it and kept his foot on the gas. We must have been going more than eighty miles an hour. As the Jeep flew, I felt both petrified and more alive than I ever had before. I began to hope that we would escape.

Sparks crackled and spat from under the Cherokee as we started to cross the train tracks. Shawna Lee suddenly said, "Sara, I don't want to die."

I turned back to face her and said, "You are not going to die." She fastened her seat belt; I heard the loud click as it engaged. Then we crashed into a tree.

I was in a coma for three days—at one point, the doctors had to shock my heart to restart it. My right arm and ribs were a broken mess.

The wreck was so severe that I found out later it had taken the Jaws of Life fifty minutes to get me out of the car. Ernie was lucky to walk away with only a broken thumb. Seth completely shattered one knee. Shawna Lee, the only one of us wearing a seat belt, died immediately on impact.

Seth was charged with manslaughter and sent to juvenile hall.

GG supplied a limousine, free of charge, to transport me and Shawna Lee's family to the funeral and burial. Shawna Lee's dad was a veteran, which meant she could be buried at River-side National Cemetery, with a short gun salute fired off in her honor. I will always regret the fact that, because of my broken arm, I was unable to place my right hand over my heart as a show of respect for my dear friend, who trusted me as much as I had trusted her.

The accident and its aftermath opened the door to an investigation into my mother's treatment of me. The fact that I was hanging out with these kids in an adult's apartment raised the suspicion of the officers, considering I was only fifteen. My mom went through the familiar motions. She told them I was suicidal and a runaway and that she had tried but could not control me. Tests showed that I had contracted two sexually transmitted diseases, so I had to admit to being sexually active. I revealed nothing about GG or his trafficking of me.

My mom told Social Services that she used to take drugs but had stopped a long time ago and had put her life back together. She said she was hoping to move to a new neighborhood with me so that we could start over. Lies, nothing but lies, yet Social Services believed her as usual.

When I started the fall semester, a teacher called Social Services after spotting scars and bruises from one of my mother's beatings on my arms and legs. A representative came to the house and, after interviewing Mom and me, decided that I should be in foster care.

I was placed in three foster homes and ran away from each. At one, the mother announced to the other children that I had STDs, so they should stay away from me, and that I'd better disinfect the bathroom with Clorox every time I used it. Social Services did not bother to follow up after the third time. All the placements were in private houses in a lower-middle-class neighborhood of Riverside County that was nicer than Rubidoux.

By now I had been a part of GG's stable for two years and I had become too jaded to fit into a normal household; the life I'd been leading had begun to inform my perception of everyday activities and interfere with my ability to consider myself a "regular" person. I had come to think of a bathroom as the place you go to in order to get ready for sex. Diamond and the other women had taught me to wash with a cloth and warm water before working. I would look at myself in the mirror, check out my face and my small breasts, and think, "Okay, here we go again." I'd take a deep breath and try to remove myself from the experience. The beds provided in foster homes were often kid-sized, and because I was tall, my legs would hang over the edge. I couldn't relax enough to imagine a bed as simply a place to sleep, as opposed to a site for sexual activity. I would toss and turn, images of sex acts flitting through my mind. Comfort was an alien state.

5

On Thanksgiving Day, I found someone to help fill the hole that Shawna Lee's death had left in my life. His name was Johnny Otis and I met him at a party thrown by Jackie, a friend from the neighborhood.

Jackie was like a wildflower, springing up here, there, and everywhere. She was unruly, colorful, and fun. She was a few years older than me, and her parents were never home. She and her sister did whatever they wanted.

My sixteenth birthday was coming around in January. When I met Johnny, I thought he was older than I was, but he actually turned out to be two months younger. I was aflutter at the sight of him at the party. At first we played eye tag, each wanting to look at the other, but not wanting to be caught looking. He was wearing an LA Raiders trench coat. The coat, along with the way he listened when I spoke and looked into my eyes, made him seem more like a mature man than a boy my age. He was cute, not gorgeous, but his easygoing manner made him appear more handsome than he was.

A few days later, a guy who had been at Jackie's invited us all to go to his place for another party, which turned out to be a turning point in my life. Jackie was a voluptuous girl with wavy blond hair, blue eyes, and big lips. The guys liked teasing her, saying she was a white girl who wanted to be Black. She used Black slang and mostly hung out with Black girls and guys. She blossomed in the light of male attention.

Snoop Dogg's *Doggystyle* played in the background. I had come to the party with Bernadette, whom I'd met at one of my foster homes. We sat playing dominoes, listening to the music and laughing as the dominoes were slammed on the kitchen table. Some of the guys smoked weed and drank. There were about fifteen of them altogether; Jackie, Bernadette, and I were the only women. The guys came and went as the night progressed, and they'd whisper and pass cash to one another. There was a lot of fist bumping and back patting. One guy took a seat near a corner, facing the front door and holding a big gun, as if on guard.

Jackie began loudly teasing the guys, challenging them. "What you gonna do? You ain't gonna do nothing! Y'all talkin', but you ain't doing nothing."

She was inviting the guys to run a train on her. A train is where a group of men line up to take turns having sex with the woman waiting at the end of the line.

Jackie allowed it all to happen with bravado. She pointed at the guys one at a time and said, "I can handle you, and then you, and then you. Can you handle me?"

Seven or eight guys were lined up in the hallway leading to the bathroom where she was waiting. The scene triggered something in me. I was put off by Jackie's casual, overly sexualized behavior. She was well built and she proudly flaunted her figure, but by now I thought of sex as something to be borne like a disease.

I sat and chatted with Johnny and the others, watching as if from afar. I had seen a train many times before, not with Jackie, but with other girls. Even though they appeared to want and invite the sex, and it was different from the unwelcome encounters I had with Johns, something about it made me feel sad. I was still very shaken up about Shawna Lee, but I was also upset to see men so willing to use Jackie for their pleasure, without any intimacy or regard for her. That night, I saw myself in Jackie.

Somebody said they wanted some weed, and to get away from the depressing atmosphere, I jumped up and said, "I'm going to make a call. I can go get some."

I needed to get out of the house and into the fresh air. Sometimes, at night, when I was at GG's or home with Mom, I would stand outside for a while looking up at the moon and stars. I would tell myself, "Keep your eyes on the light. It makes the darkness disappear." I wanted to go outside now and get lost in the sky. I made a subconscious decision to change my life that night.

Johnny accompanied me outside. As we walked up the street and easily talked about this and that, I felt at peace. We returned and smoked weed. Not long afterward, people began dispersing.

Bernadette and I got up to leave together. I didn't want to go back to the foster home Bernadette and I had once shared, even though I knew our former foster mother would take me in, or to my Mom's. I didn't have anywhere else to go except GG's, but after seeing what had happened to Jackie, I didn't feel like rushing there either.

Johnny said to me, "Do you want me to drop you off at home?"

I said, "Okay."

Since I didn't want to let Johnny know about GG, I had him leave me and Bernadette up the street.

He said, "I'll see you later."

Bernadette and I set out on foot to crash at one of the motels GG operated from. When we got there, Bernadette began talking to a guy who was standing outside. The next thing I knew, a car pulled up and Johnny jumped out.

"Sara, what are you doing here?"

I was so surprised to see him all I could say was "Johnny?"

"Come here."

I went over to him.

"I thought you were going home."

I didn't have to say anything. He seemed to understand. He said, "Get in the car."

He took me to his house. Inside, he hid me behind his trench coat and herded me into his room, "Quick, quick, hide!"

He made me lie between the edge of his waterbed and the wall while he went out to talk to his mom so she wouldn't get suspicious or come barging in.

He came back and gave me boxers and a tank top. As we got into the bed, he said, "I'm not going to try anything with you, so don't worry."

We fell asleep side by side. At some point in the night, he woke, and tapped me on the shoulder. "You asleep?"

"Not anymore. Are you?"

"Can I hold you?"

I thought to myself, "Wow. He is the kind of person who will ask somebody that."

"Yes," I said.

No one had ever asked me for permission to touch me, hold me, or kiss me. Right then and there, I fell in love with him.

Johnny and I became inseparable. He had the sweetest smile, wore his hair in a ponytail, and had a little mustache. He had good manners, holding the door open for me, pulling out a chair for me to sit on. I adored him. He had a manly way of making me feel he could take care of me. We started making plans to run away together and find a place to live.

Soon Johnny's mom knew about me, so sometimes I stayed there with them. I kept up my old habit of always checking in with my mom. I told her I had a boyfriend and gave her Johnny's number. She called Mrs. Otis and threatened to report her to the police for harboring a foster care runaway. Mom was a little afraid of Social Services. With Mrs. Otis now rattled, the only place left for me to go was GG's, but I had decided to put an end to that. Johnny understood and supported me. He took me to the house of the uncle of a friend of his, a man named James Earl Hampton.

James Earl was bad news. He already had a long arrest record and had served several jail terms. He had recently been released from one of them. He was selling crack out of the house and had guns lying all over the place. He scared me more than anyone I'd ever met, so I did my best to stay out of his way, but I could always feel his eyes on me. He seized every opportunity to brag to me about his criminal record and escapades, which, according to him, included murders and other violent acts. By the way he carried himself, I knew these were likely not empty boasts.

One day, when Johnny wasn't around, I was busy scrubbing the bathtub with Comet. I felt a presence behind me and turned around. James Earl stood there watching me. The hairs on my neck rose, I was frightened to my core.

"You really love that li'l nigga Johnny, don't you?"

With my heart in my throat, I said, "Yeah."

He smirked and said, "If I killed that muthafucka, your ass won't be able to love him no more."

I didn't know what to do or say. Thankfully he left. I continued scrubbing, but my mind turned to getting out of there as soon as possible. I knew we had to leave. I was afraid he was now going to kill Johnny just to prove to me how bad he was. When Johnny got back, I told him we had to find some money quickly and leave town; I couldn't continue living this way. I told him how badly I wanted to go straight and for us to find an apartment to move into together. He said the problem was he didn't have enough money for an apartment. He was running errands for James Earl, doing a little of this and that, but he promised he would begin to save.

I said, "I'll get a job at a McDonald's and we can save that too."

"It's still going to take us a while to get enough for a month's rent and security."

I sat there next to him, knowing he was right. I felt helpless and urgently wanted to find a way out of this mess. I knew in my heart that James Earl could hurt us just for the hell of it. I knew he could get Johnny tied up in serious trouble. Out of the blue a bizarre thought occurred to me: "GG has tons of cash. I'm going to ask him to help us."

Johnny looked at me with interest. "How much do you think he's got?"

I said, "He always has a few thousand in his wallet. If I get him in a good mood, I'm sure he'll give me some."

Later, when the police questioned me after my arrest, they kept filling in the blanks in my story for it to make sense to them. I grew frustrated trying to explain to them that there never was a conversation mapping out what was going to happen or how things would go. They wanted a succession of events plotted neatly; they wanted reason or logic when there was none.

I would say to them, "No, that's not how it was. I wasn't aware of a plan. I didn't know what was about to go down." They refused to believe me.

I still don't know why things turned out the way they did. As far as I can guess, Johnny must have told James Earl that I was close to GG. Everyone had heard of Felix Limousines and knew he was one of the richest businessmen in town. I don't know this for sure, but I assume that, based on what I said to Johnny and what he told James Earl, they hatched a plan to rob and kill GG, using me as bait.

Today I have to remind myself that Johnny was sixteen, as was I. We were kids. I still don't understand why he involved James Earl, as we were both desperate to escape from him.

A day after my conversation with Johnny, he told me James Earl wanted me to call GG and ask him for money. I asked why James Earl had anything to do with our business, and Johnny told me not to worry. They had figured out a way for GG to give me the money even if he didn't want to and needed me to execute the plan.

As I got into his car, James Earl handed a small revolver to Johnny, who passed it to me through the open window, saying, "Be careful. The safety's off."

I wondered about it for a second but didn't question him about it or try to refuse it. After all, we were in front of James Earl, of whom I was terrified. I didn't dwell on the gun. Not yet. I put it in my purse, thinking they were giving it to me for self-protection. I had never held a gun like this, but I had certainly seen a lot of them. I didn't for a moment think, "Oh no, they're getting ready to try to kill somebody. I'd better call the police."

James Earl said, "I want you to get GG to take you some-place where you can be alone."

That was the first thing that struck me as very odd.

"Why?"

"Don't worry why, we'll be following you. Just get him somewhere and we'll take care of the rest."

I understood now that there was to be a robbery and that I was supposed to facilitate it. As with sex with Johns, I disassociated myself from what was happening. It did not occur to me that anyone would get hurt. I thought Johnny and James Earl were simply scheming to grab and run off with GG's wallet.

James Earl and Johnny drove me to a pay phone outside a hamburger stand.

James Earl said, "Call GG."

I called GG.

As improbable as it might seem, nothing about what had happened so far raised a red flag for me. I was accustomed to men in my environment bragging about being "killas," shooting, and getting shot at as if they were talking about eating ice cream cones. They loved to order females around, and for the most part, we just did what they said.

What I knew when I made the call to GG and asked to see him was that I was only going to help make the robbery possible, and they would take care of business after that. I didn't feel bad, because GG had a ton of ill-gotten money and I knew that whatever he was carrying on him wasn't going to make a dent.

Things started to go wrong pretty quickly.

Instead of GG coming to get me, he sent Big Mama. I reluctantly got into the car with her, and she drove me to GG's house. I kept looking back but I didn't see Johnny and James Earl following me. When we got to the house, GG wasn't there. Nor was there any sign of Johnny and James Earl when I looked out a window. I had no idea what to do next.

As I was sneaking out the front door to leave, Big Mama came up behind me and asked me where I was going. I told her I was just running down the street to get cigarettes. She must have thought that odd because I'd never smoked before, but she didn't say anything. I left the house and walked so fast I was practically running. I flagged down a car and asked the driver please to take me to a store, any store. He stared at me weirdly but drove on as I forced myself to make small talk with him. He dropped me off at a liquor store.

I ran inside to the pay phone and paged Johnny. James Earl called me right back and asked me where I was. I told him things were all messed up: GG wasn't where he should have been. I gave him my location. It took him and Johnny a little while to get there. As I waited, I paced nervously back and forth. Everything seemed off. I was beginning to have a bad feeling about what I had unwittingly gotten myself into. I hoped James Earl would say, "Forget it."

By the time they arrived, I had worked myself up into a state.

"Where were you? I kept looking for you and you weren't there. I don't know what I'm supposed to do now."

All James Earl said was "We lost you."

I said, "GG wasn't at the house. I told Big Mama I was going to get cigarettes. I don't even smoke."

James Earl replied, "You called him, and he told you to come. That means he's expecting you, so get in the car. I'm taking you back."

"I don't think we should do this today," I said.

James Earl was insistent: "He's expecting you."

Johnny was oddly quiet. He seemed unable to look me in the eye. Instead of thinking I was being set up, I became worried that Johnny was afraid that James Earl was going to hurt him if I didn't do as I was told.

James Earl went into the liquor store and bought a pack of Camels. He took one cigarette out of the pack and put the rest in my purse.

We got back in his car. James Earl handed me a pager.

"When I page you, I want you to call me back without making GG suspicious and tell me where you are."

Johnny and James Earl dropped me in front of GG's house, and I went back inside. If Big Mama thought I was acting strange, she kept it to herself. I sat on a couch, apprehensive about what might happen next. I tried to smile and look relaxed, even though I was feeling anything but. I kept taking the pager out and looking at it and putting it back.

About five minutes after I'd sat down, the phone rang in the house. A woman answered it. I heard her say, "Yeah, Daddy, she's here. I'll tell her." She hung up, turned to me, and said, "Daddy's outside waiting for you."

I tried to look calm and nonchalant as I walked to the door. I said, "Thank you." The doorknob felt like cold fire as I turned it. I walked toward the car feeling as if it had left an imprint on my palm.

GG was in his cream-colored Jaguar. I snuck a peek to the left and right to see if James Earl and Johnny were lurking. I didn't see them anywhere. The way this was going made no sense to me. I was shaking inside, but I tried to steady myself.

"Sara, beautiful little Sara," GG said. "I'm going to take you to a movie tonight."

I made myself smile and nod. I got into his car and looked out the window at the sky. As the car pulled away from the curb, it seemed as if the stars were following us.

As *Blue Chips* began, I felt the pager vibrate. I excused myself and left to call James Earl from the pay phone by the ladies' room to let him know where GG and I were. He said that after the movie I should get GG to a motel room and let him know which one and the room number. He would come to the door and knock once. I was to open it and leave the rest to him and Johnny. I said okay and asked to speak to Johnny. James Earl put him on the phone. Even though Johnny was strangely reticent, when he said, "Don't worry, we got you," I felt better. Still there was something odd in his voice that stuck with me.

James grabbed the phone from Johnny and said, "Get GG to a motel," and hung up. After the movie, when GG walked into the liquor store, I checked the pager. I saw that James Earl had paged "187." What the fuck? I knew from listening to rap that the number referred to murder in the California Penal Code. I was afraid it meant that James Earl had done something to Johnny. GG had one of those big, unwieldy, old-fashioned car phones. I grabbed it and dialed. James Earl answered. I told him to put Johnny on the line. He said, "No. You can't talk to him right now."

I kept an eye on the liquor store door and pleaded with him to please let me talk to Johnny.

He said, "He's cool. He's with me. I need you to do what I'm telling you to do. You can talk to him after that. Page me when you get to the motel."

I whispered, "Okay, James," and hung up as GG came strolling out of the store, got back in the car, and handed me the bag of liquor to hold.

At the Dynasty Suites, when GG left the car to pay for the room, I looked at the pager and saw that James Earl had paged "187" again. I called him from the car phone. James Earl answered, and I again told him to put Johnny on the phone.

James Earl laughed and said, "What you sound so scared for? Until you do what I say, you ain't gon' speak to him. And if you don't do what I tell you, you ain't never gon' speak to him."

I said, "Why do you keep sending me 187?"

He said, "Because I need you to shoot and rob GG." He hung up.

I can identify the precise moment when I realized that I hated GG. It was at Shawna Lee's burial, graveside, as the gun salute rang out. I started talking to him in my mind. "GG, because of you, I've had sex with hundreds of strangers. Because of that, I've helped to pay for your houses. Every man who has slept with me has added to your privilege." I turned toward the parking lot: I had even helped to pay for the limousines that GG had provided so that we could send Shawna Lee off in style. Glossy black long cars waiting in line to take us home. I had contributed to everything that made GG powerful. I hated that the community applauded his status and the image he projected. Most of all, I couldn't stand the fact that I had allowed myself to be tricked into helping him attain that image. Yet I was forced to acknowledge a painful truth: at that very moment I was wearing clothes and shoes he had given me. And, as much as I hated having sex with him and all the other men, and what he stood for, I knew no other way to live.

For as long as I can remember, I've had a tendency to avoid being in the present. When I'm present, I'm in my body, and when I'm in my body, I have to acknowledge my scars. To acknowledge my scars means that I have to remember how I got them, and that means I have to hold myself accountable for taking part in the circumstances that caused them. I am now a forty-four-year-old woman and I still sometimes feel unwhole, unclean, insecure, ashamed, and humiliated because of what happened when I was a child. When I'm feeling particularly bad, I take a shower. I run it as hot as I can stand it and scrub myself with a washcloth. I picture all the dirt and pain that has stuck to me during my lifetime swirling down the drain. I cry and cry, and let the tears join the water spiraling downward.

The night I killed GG and drove away barefoot, I found James Earl and Johnny standing by the pay phone at the gas station where James Earl had told me to meet them. Seeing them brought me back to myself. I began shaking. I put the car into park, left the key in the ignition and the engine running, opened the door, and ran to them. Out of breath and on

the verge of tears, I said, "I shot him. Oh my God. I think he's
dead!"

All James Earl said was "Gimme everything you've got."

"My shoes and purse. I forgot them!"

"Don't worry about that. Where's the money and gun?"

"In the car," I said.

He strolled over to the Jaguar without a backward glance at
me, got in, and drove off. I was so numb, I couldn't cry, even
though I wanted to.

"Is he dead?" Johnny asked.

"I don't know," I answered. "He was on the ground and I
just left him there."

"It's going to be okay," Johnny told me.

We got into James Earl's car and left. Johnny pulled up to a
house I had never been to before. I saw GG's Jaguar sitting in
the driveway. Nothing was making sense.

"Come on, get out," Johnny said, motioning with his hand.
My feet hit the cold concrete, and I shivered as I followed him
toward the house, entering it through the open garage door.

I went to the bathroom, where I locked the door and leaned
against it. That is when I began to weep into my hands. I didn't
want anyone to hear me cry, so I sobbed silently. I didn't want
to be called a punk or a bitch. I stood in front of the sink and
washed my hands and face. I took a deep breath, gripped the
doorknob, opened the door, and put on a smile even though I
felt that if I moved too quickly, I might crack and break.

James Earl and Johnny, big grins on their faces, approached
me. James Earl tossed two hundred-dollar bills at me, and said,
"There was fifteen hundred in the wallet. Here's two hundred.
That's all you."

I handed the two hundred dollars straight to Johnny who,
I later found out, used the entire amount to buy drugs from
James Earl to try to sell and make a profit.

My eyes pleaded with Johnny to acknowledge what I was feeling—scared, confused, conflicted, and in need of comfort—but he didn't pick up on my cues and left with James Earl. "We out," they said cheerfully as they walked away.

Later, when Johnny and James Earl came back, I overheard them talking. They said they had wiped the car down, stripped it, and burned GG's ID.

"Sara, smile. Come on, baby, smile." Johnny's voice snatched my attention as he came into the bedroom.

When I was younger, my mom told me she wanted to name me Papillon, the word for butterfly in French. She would crack herself up explaining why she didn't follow through with that idea. "I didn't want you to go through life getting called Happy Nappy, or Happy Pappy." She heard a song by Hall and Oates called "Sara Smile" and went with that instead.

"Okay," I said, and tried to live up to my name.

Johnny and James Earl took me back to James's house, where I fell asleep.

The next morning, they both came into the room I had slept in. I was sitting on the side of the bed, staring at the wall, trying to find the will to stand.

They told me that they had heard on the radio that GG was dead. James Earl announced, "I'm putting you on a Greyhound bus to Arizona until this blows over. But first, you gotta call your mom. Tell her you were at a motel with GG. There was a break-in, two masked men came in, one guy threw you down to the floor and put his foot on your back so you couldn't see anything, but then he told you to leave. You ran out without your shoes and purse and don't know what happened. Just say that, nothing else."

With trembling fingers, I dialed. My mom answered. "Mom?" I said.

She replied, "Where are you?"

It was as if I had lost my ability to speak. I kept repeating, "Mom, Mom."

"Sara, are you with Johnny?" she asked.

My mouth wasn't working. I couldn't remember the words I was supposed to say. James Earl gestured to me to get off the phone.

"I gotta go, Mom," I said, and hung up.

Something in my expression, and in my inability to follow his instructions, must have caused James Earl to say, "I don't trust you alone on the bus," before he and Johnny left the room and shut the door.

When I came out to use the bathroom, they were both sitting in the hallway, as if guarding the room. James Earl told me not to close the bathroom door all the way. I did my business and headed toward the kitchen. James Earl asked me where I was going. I said, "I just want to get something to drink."

James Earl nodded at Johnny, who jumped up and said he would get me some food and drink, but I should go back in the room and stay there. And that was the way it went until the next day, when James Earl came in and told me to get up and follow him because he was taking me somewhere. I asked if Johnny could come.

"No," he said.

By now, I felt as if I had entered the Twilight Zone. I would think, "I have to take a step," and I would look down and see GG falling dead at my feet. Then he would vanish, and I'd try to take the next step. The same thing would happen.

James Earl pushed me into his car, blasted rap music, and drove me about an hour away to Long Beach. I don't think we said one word to each other, nor did I have a coherent thought during the entire drive. We pulled up in front of a small apartment building, where he knocked at one of the doors. A Black woman who looked to be in her thirties opened it. I don't believe I could have recognized her if I had passed her on the street an hour later. James Earl said to the woman, who did not seem thrilled to see us, "Hold her in the bedroom. Don't let her out. Don't let her use the phone. I'll be back." He pushed me inside. I heard the bedroom door lock, and then, a few seconds later, his car drive away. I began knocking on the door and yelling, "Miss, can I please use your phone? Please?"

When I realized that was not going to happen, I lay down on the bed and tried to force myself to sleep. Locked in the bedroom, I had no idea there was a manhunt under way for GG's murderer.

Reading the reports about GG's murder investigation today is like reading about something that happened to someone else. I learned that a staff member at the motel had heard the gunshot, found GG's body, and called the police. It didn't take long for them to find my shoes, my purse, and my ID inside the room. Those were the most important pieces of evidence, along with the motel's record of the license plate of GG's Jaguar.

Inside my purse, retrieved at the motel, the detectives found lipstick, Ban roll-on deodorant, an eye shadow compact, a tube of mascara, and an employment application from a local McDonald's restaurant.

The police discovered that the car was registered to a woman named Tonya Gillam who, when they called her, said she was GG's girlfriend. I had never heard her name before. Using my ID, they combed through state records and learned that I had recently run away from a foster home. They also tracked down my mom's number and telephoned her.

I can almost hear and see my mother in the words of the report made by Homicide Investigator Sergeant Mark Boyer of the Riverside Police Department:

Mrs. Kruzan told me that her daughter was a habitual runaway. She gave me her boyfriend Johnny Otis's name and address. She further told me that if I was to call his house, I should ask to speak to his mother because, along with her daughter, her daughter's boyfriend would not tell the truth. I then asked her if she knew who drove a white Jaguar? She said, "That's the pimp!" I asked if she knew his name. She said, "GG. I don't know his real name." She described him to me as a tall Black man who wore a lot of jewelry and long hair which looked like it had come out of curlers. We then contacted Mrs. Otis, who said Johnny wasn't there, and she had no idea where Kruzan was.

The following morning, I knocked on the bedroom door and again begged the woman to let me use her phone to call my mom. I told her my mom would call the cops if I didn't check in with her. I was on my knees, pleading. Finally, she opened it, set the phone on the floor, closed the door again, and snapped at me to hurry up. I dialed Mom's number.

When she picked up, I told her James Earl's concocted story. I said I was scared and hiding out because I was afraid that the two men might come after me. She kept asking me where I was. I told her I couldn't say and hung up.

The woman must have been listening. She opened the door, grabbed the phone, and locked me inside again.

Detective Boyer states that my mom called and told him that she had received a call from me. She repeated the story I had given her. He told her if I called again to try to get me to meet her somewhere.

James Earl arrived early to get me the next day. He brought me back to his house and told me he was going out, had business to take care of, and would be back later. He said no one else was there and that I should not leave the house. I checked and it was true: nobody was home. I worked up the courage to run up the street to the pay phone across from a 7-Eleven store, and called my mom. She said the police were looking for me. I took a deep breath and told her where the 7-Eleven was. I said I would meet her and the police in front of the parking lot.

I left the phone booth, hid behind James Earl's house, and peeked out at the street. Eventually, a car drove by, and I saw my mom's profile in the back seat. It parked in front of the 7-Eleven. I began to cry. I didn't know what to do. I was afraid of James Earl. I was worried about Johnny. I lost my nerve and went back into the house. James hadn't returned yet. I went to the room, lay down on the bed, and cried myself to sleep.

Later that night, when James Earl came back, he resumed his drug dealing. Customers came and went. I heard music, laughing, partying. I remained in the room, trying to block out flashbacks to the motel room and GG's last moments, wondering where Johnny was.

Early the next morning, I was trying to get up the nerve to call my mom again when I heard a car pull up. From the bedroom window, I saw Johnny in the car. I ran outside. Johnny had a strange look, as though he knew something that he wasn't telling me. He said, "Come on, Sara, we've got to go."

"Where are we going?"

"Never mind, get in the car."

"Okay, I have to get my shoes," I said.

I was barefoot, so I turned to run back inside just as undercover detectives in an unmarked car arrived. They drove up to the front of the house, jumped out of their vehicle, and yelled, "Freeze! You're under arrest!"

Because the detectives were wearing civilian clothes, I at first didn't process what was happening. I kept walking toward the house to get my shoes.

"I said, freeze, you're under arrest."

I turned around, faced the detective, and politely asked, "I'm sorry, are you talking to me?"

"I am," he replied as if addressing an idiot, before binding my wrists with zip ties and pushing me toward the unmarked car.

From the car window, I could see the cops talking with Johnny; I was sure that he was explaining and fixing it.

I heard him say, "Can I say something to her before you take her away?"

One of the cops said, "Go ahead."

Johnny came up to the window, looked me in the eye, and whispered, "You better not tell them nothing."

I felt a chill of fear and had my first moment of doubt about him. I put my head down and said, "Okay."

6

"Did you shoot and kill George Gilbert Howard?"

"Who?"

It took me a moment to realize they meant GG and that GG derived from George Gilbert. I had never questioned it.

My focus came and went. *CHiPs* was a popular TV series I used to watch as a kid about two motorcycle cops, Frank, a.k.a. "Ponch," and Jon, who were friendly and harmless. Even though my real-life experience with cops so far was that they were usually not very friendly and the community I was a part of steered clear of them, I kept telling myself, "Maybe these guys are like the *CHiPs* cops." It certainly never occurred to me that they would try to send me to jail for the rest of my life.

I was in a small cold room. I was tired. I was handcuffed. They kept getting up and leaving me alone in the room.

The first cop had introduced himself as Sergeant Detective Boyer. He had reddish hair and a mustache and did most of the talking. The second had a close-cropped military-style haircut and stern bearing. He was Detective Ron San Filippo.

Sergeant Boyer looked a little like a cop I had once had sex with in Los Angeles. He had shown up in his own car wearing his uniform. I got into the car, saw the uniform, and went to get right out. He said, "Wait a minute, don't go," unzipped his pants, reached in and plucked out one of his pubic hairs, which he handed me along with the twenty-dollar bill he was paying me to receive a blow job, as proof that he wouldn't arrest me.

I could hear some of what they were saying, and I'd attempt to answer even as my mind wandered in multiple directions. Although they had read me my rights in the car, I still didn't understand that I could remain silent or demand to have a lawyer present. I was intelligent enough, but also naive. First, I repeated James Earl's false narrative, but Sergeant Boyer self-confidently interrupted me, and told me I was lying because the cameras at the motel showed otherwise. The police claimed to have reviewed the film and seen that only GG and I had entered the motel room. Later, at my trial, I learned that this claim was fabricated. To be sure, there was a security camera at the motel, but the film had been recorded over by the time the police looked at it. Sitting there in the interrogation room, however, I believed the detective and broke down quickly. I told them the truth and felt a weight lift from me. Relieved, I started telling them about James Earl, but they kept interrupting me to insist that they knew I had acted on my own. Leaving the room, they told me the DA was going to come to speak to me, but he never came.

They left me alone for a few hours, then returned to put metal cuffs on my wrists and take me to Riverside Juvenile Hall, a gray concrete building behind a barbed-wire fence. A probation officer named Pearl Graves booked and processed me; she assigned me to Girls Unit 6/7. Because of my high-security profile, I was remanded to a restricted area. I was given the standard uniform: green khaki pants, a T-shirt, and Velcro-fastened sneakers. High-security kids like me were issued bright yellow T-shirts; lower-security girls and boys wore pink and blue T-shirts with their green pants.

I was taken to a small cell near the cop shop (the probation officer's desk). It was approximately seven feet by ten. All it contained was a single bed, a tiny sink, a toilet, and a small cubby. Along with others wearing yellow shirts, I was locked inside for most of the day. The rest of the kids in pink and blue could come and go from the dorm-style rooms they slept in. They could leave and return to their rooms at will. They ate dinner together in the cafeteria, watched TV in the dayroom, and were allowed yard time as a group.

My bed was fastened to the wall, as was the little wooden cubby for my clothes and belongings. The cell had a small, grimy window four inches wide and two feet high with a latticed metal grille affixed to the front. A camera was mounted in the corner of the ceiling, recording my every move. I was self-conscious any time I had to use the toilet. My meals were brought to the cell on a tray that was set on the cubby for me to eat alone.

Two days after my arrival, I was awakened at dawn and driven, chained and shackled, about twenty minutes away to downtown Riverside. California law states that within forty-eight hours of arrest, a defendant must be brought before a judge to be charged. As I sat in the holding cell in the courthouse on a cot, my eyes lingered on the paint peeling from the walls, then traveled down to the dirty cement floor. Every time I inhaled, the shackles on my ankles jingled. Apart from this sound, the place was eerily quiet. Soon I could also hear the click of footsteps getting louder as they approached the cell. Its door was unlocked, and an officer told me to follow him.

I stood, adjusted the waist chains, checked that my too-long pants were folded at the hem above my shoes so I would not trip, and shuffled behind the officer into the courtroom. The lawyer assigned to me, a tall thin man I had never met named Robert Oblachinski, was waiting at one table. He looked to be in his forties, a white man, like most of the others in the courtroom. He gestured to a seat beside him. In front of us, Judge Patrick Magers was sitting high up on a dais. The Riverside deputy district attorney, Timothy Freer, sat at a table adjacent to ours. I heard my name announced, along with some numbers, and then the two lawyers and the judge began to talk and argue. Mr. Oblachinski had arrived in court with no knowledge of the case. Detective Boyer was the only witness called. He spoke about me as if I weren't there, in a tone that bordered on hostility.

When Mr. Oblachinski, who quickly looked over the reports, brought up the subject of James Earl, the DA convinced the judge to disallow any mention of him, since there was no tangible evidence he was involved. I began to cry as I heard my name being repeated over and over in connection with the events. There was no further discussion about James Earl, and it was clear that they all thought shooting GG was my idea. Nobody looked at me. Nothing was explained to me or asked of me. I may as well not have been there. As invisible as I felt, I was aware of my mind wandering, as usual, away from grim unpleasantness and hurt.

Mr. Oblachinski nudged my shoulder. "Do you agree, Sara?" He opened his eyes wide at me and gave an almost imperceptible nod, intimating the right answer.

"Yes, I agree," I responded, without knowing what I was agreeing to.

I tried to smile at Judge Magers, who at least looked directly at me before he said, "Thank you," and stood up to leave.

An officer escorted me to the holding cell to await transport back to juvenile hall. I did not comprehend what had happened. The ride back was fast. I didn't feel like eating; I just wanted to go to bed. The chains were taken off me, which gave me a fleeting sensation of freedom until I was asked to disrobe for a strip search. My stomach, which had been cramping for months, hurt more than usual. I told the officer on duty, who promised to get me an appointment to see a doctor. I sat on the toilet and tried to urinate the pain away. I felt a pulling inside me, almost like a tearing. I stood up and got ready for bed, lay down on the thin mattress, covered myself with the rough sheet and wool blanket, curled up into a ball, closed my eyes, and cried myself to sleep.

My next court visit was three months later, for a 707 fitness hearing to determine whether I should be tried as a juvenile or an adult. I was still a minor, but due to the severity of the crime I was accused of, murder in the first degree, a 707 hearing was mandatory. On June 20, 1994, I appeared before the Honorable Timothy J. Heaslett. The hearing was more or less a replica of the arraignment, except that this judge was a different, older, and less pleasant white man, and Mr. Oblachinski had asked to be relieved from defending my case after the arraignment. I was assigned a new lawyer named David Gunn, whom I had met at juvenile hall a few days before the hearing. Mr. Gunn was a kind man who did his best to explain to me the implications of the decision the judge would be making.

The judge found me unfit for juvenile court under 707 because of what he called "the degree of criminal sophistication exhibited" in my case. The judge asserted that my crime "was planned and premeditated" and decided that I should be tried in an adult court.

After the 707 hearing, I was finally given a full physical by a pediatrician. It was discovered that I was suffering from pelvic inflammatory disease. The doctor's notes in my legal file read: ". . . patient handcuffed and chain around waist—difficult to expose patient. Abdomen soft, tender to percussion. Cervical tenderness. Diagnosis: Depression, PID, Trichomoniasis. Treatment: Doxycycline, Cefotetan, Flagyl, Erythromycin, Elavil." It was as if the distress I felt and the abuse I had suffered over the years were announcing their physical presence.

Over the next nine months I spent at juvenile hall, if I wasn't studying, I tried to find some other way to occupy myself. Sometimes I asked if I could mop the floors. This might seem odd, but if you imagine being locked in a cell all day at age sixteen, any activity that allowed you to leave your cell was welcome. It felt good to be assigned a chore. The staff usually agreed to my request because it saved them from having to do the job themselves. The hallway floor was dusty and dull and always looked scuffed, so I challenged myself to try to make it pretty. I would spend hours dusting, sweeping, mopping, and waxing the emerald-green linoleum until it shone.

All told, I spent a year at juvenile hall among a rotating group of girls and boys who had somehow fallen afoul of the law, and a mostly unchanging roster of staff. While some of the corrections officers treated me and the other children as if we were evil incarnate, Pearl Graves, the woman who had processed me on arrival, never did. During my time in her charge, Ms. Graves, a pretty, caramel-colored woman, provided a kind of mothering I had never experienced and desperately needed. She dried my tears many a time after a difficult visit from my mother, who, having become a born-again Christian, would urge me to pray while accusing me of being godless. Mom spent her visits complaining about all the unfair things that were happening in her life, or she would tell me she was feeling sick and it was my fault. She seemed to think I was deliberately attempting to hurt her by having gotten into this situation. These visits left me emotionally overwrought. I would return to my cell, where I was strip-searched after each visit, a procedure that triggered memories of being trafficked on the street. Sometimes I became so upset that the staff put me on suicide watch.

Although Ms. Graves worked at the facility and represented authority during my incarceration there, I came to regard her as a friend. Whenever I left my cell, whether for an attorney meeting, group therapy, a court appearance, or a family visit, I had to be placed in restraints. Ms. Graves was the one who usually wrapped the shackles around my ankles and the chains around my waist. It didn't bother me because I knew it was her job. She invited me to join the girls' circle in group therapy, in which anywhere from ten to twenty of us were encouraged to talk about issues that troubled us. We were allowed to scream or stamp our feet to express our frustration at the circumstances in which we found ourselves; sometimes we would laugh as we let loose our pain and anger. At the end of these sessions, Ms. Graves gave us grapes and Cheetos. She assured me that someday, when this was all over, we would meet, have lunch, and she would bring Cheetos and grapes. Twenty years later, that happened.

One day, I asked Ms. Graves if I could take the garbage out to the bins in the small backyard of the facility. This sounds like a little thing, but it was prohibited for anyone wearing a yellow T-shirt to go there. The other kids took turns doing it as a chore. None of them ever wanted to, and here I was, pining to take out the garbage. The yard was fenced in, but behind the fence was freedom, meaning it was seriously off limits to someone who was considered a flight risk. Ms. Graves understood that I had no intention of running away; I just wanted to do something normal so that I could see myself as equal to the others. I wanted to be trusted, even for a moment.

I could see her thinking it over, and she agreed, but first she made me change into a pink T-shirt. Then she told me that if I tried to run away, she would take her shoe off and hit me in the head with it. I grabbed the big bag proudly. It was a little heavy, but I strutted out to the garbage bins with that bag and took my time. Then I ran back inside. Ms. Graves gave me a hug and quickly took the pink T-shirt back before any of the other officers saw it. I will never forget the sensation of putting the bag in the bin, standing outside for a moment feeling free, feeling ordinary.

As I had earlier in my life, I was able to immerse myself in my studies, hoping for knowledge or wisdom that might lead me to feel good about myself—and afford me glimpses of a possible bright future.

The dayroom was on the same floor as my cell. When I arrived, I was given the option of taking classes there in the mornings, which I enthusiastically signed up for. I grew to love my teacher, Miss Eckess. She had graying hair cut very short, and she always wore plaid button-up shirts tucked into jeans cinched with a cowboy-style buckle belt. When I was in her class, I never felt that I was in juvenile hall waiting to be tried for murder. She treated me as the sixteen-year-old girl I was. She told me that I could graduate high school and eventually go to college. She pushed me and gave me extra homework so that I could catch up.

Miss Eckess said, "If you really want to, you have the potential to graduate early, Sara. You can do it." That became my goal.

I loved going to the dayroom and picking out a volume of

the Encyclopaedia Britannica to take back to my cell to read, in addition to my schoolbooks. I worked hard and earned my high school equivalency diploma in the year I spent at juvenile hall awaiting trial. Reaching that milestone felt to me the way I imagine arriving at the summit of Mount Kilimanjaro must feel to climbers. It was a huge step forward and validation that I was not what those judges and lawyers in the courtroom thought of me. It was proof that I was capable of achieving something. Not long after my 707 hearing, I wrote an essay titled "When I Get Out of Juvenile Hall, What My Plans Are":

First off, when I get out of juvenile hall, I will definitely be thankful. I plan to go to college so I would first have to get settled, find a job, and then look into what is available for schooling. If I go to YA (Youth Authority) then my time in there would be devoted to a college degree. Depending on how long I stay. I really wouldn't mind if I had to spend a couple of years in YA because the schooling is free. It beats paying for your junior college, which I would have to attend before registering for Spelman University. So that I take advantage, once I do have my junior college completed and accepted to Spelman, I would major in social science, or take on the medical so I can get my doctrine [sic]. I want to be capable of taking care of myself, to get a man who is highly educated and prepared for life with its advantages and disadvantages. I feel that I need to be financially stable, so that when I start my family, life will be comfortable. I plan to marry before I start my family, and I want to marry a sophisticated man, so there wouldn't be a rush to tie the knot of my past.

I also want to be there for my mother. For my goal with her is to buy her own house in the country with lots of property. When I was a young girl in the days [sic], I would repeatedly tell her that I was going to do that for her when I was older. And I don't break promises!

I was seventeen by the time my trial began on May 2, 1995. The night before I was to appear in court, I tried to prepare myself to look my best by wrapping my hair around strips of toilet paper because I didn't have curlers.

David Gunn, the public defender who had also represented me in the 707 hearing, was assigned to my case. In one of a few meetings we had at juvenile hall before trial, he told me that the district attorney was offering me a plea deal of thirty years, with the possibility of time off for good behavior and the possibility of parole. Mr. Gunn advised me not to accept. He felt confident that he would get me exonerated by citing what GG had done to me at such a young age. He planned to build my defense by explaining to the court that the shooting was a result of the PTSD I had suffered as a result of having been trafficked by GG since I was thirteen. He tried his best to connect the murder to James Earl and Johnny Otis. He had them deposed, but both claimed they had not participated in the events of the night of GG's murder in any way, so they were not required to appear.

As soon as the trial began, it was clear that Mr. Gunn's reasoned approach was no match for Timothy Freer's aggressive theatrics. Mr. Gunn, as I found out when I looked him up, later went on to become a judge himself. He was a pleasant and well-meaning man who spoke to me politely, and I believe he did his best. Mr. Freer, who also became a judge, was young and fiery back then. Whenever he spoke, he was all passion and fury. Because of my age and the fact that I was female, the case received a lot of media attention. I understand now that Mr. Freer was building his career and that this was a big trial for him. In addition to the tone he used when referring to me he always looked at me with horror, as if he had just learned that I had strangled his children with my bare hands. His manner toward me, and toward Mr. Gunn, who was mild-mannered and fatherly, was dismissive.

On the days I went to court, I was awakened at 6 a.m. and ready by 7 a.m. to be transported in the sheriff's van to the Riverside County jail. Occasionally boys from juvenile hall would ride with me in the van to attend their own hearings. For the twenty minutes it took, we'd talk and giggle like the kids we were. Usually, however, I made the trip solo, and once I was taken to the holding cells, I would be one of the very few females, let alone children, in the place; the others held there awaiting trial were mostly adult males.

The cells were damp and dark, located below street level. For the walk between them and the courthouse, my ankles and waist were always shackled with chains attached to my wrists. The ankle chains were regularly too tight, which meant that the metal sometimes cut into my wrists. I had to shuffle down the long halls past the men, who whistled, catcalled, and made rude comments. Some would expose themselves to me. Once I caught a grown man masturbating furiously as I walked by. I did my best to ignore them all. Sometimes I was escorted by the guards, but mostly they would just unlock the door to my cell and point down the hall. I would do the ankle-chain shuffle down the passageway alone to get to the elevator.

When I first arrived at the jail for my trial, a man in the cell next to mine said, "Hey little girl, hey baby, who's your judge?"

"Thompson Hanks," I timidly responded.

He laughed and said, "That's fucked up, girl. Damn, who did you kill, the fuckin' president? That's Hang 'Em Hanks. He ain't no joke. You're going to get life."

I learned that J. Thompson Hanks was famous for his inability to show compassion and his readiness to hand out death and life-without-parole sentences as freely as M&M's. If you were a defendant in his courtroom, chances are you'd be convicted.

After two and a half days of preliminary motions, the trial, which lasted only five days, began. In those early motions, I had no idea that the lawyers were negotiating what could be allowed into evidence during the trial, which would determine the outcome and whether I would live the rest of my life in prison.

Hang 'Em Hanks was barely civil toward me. He never looked at me when he spoke to me. Every time he said my name or referred to me, it was with an air of disdain. One day, he announced that I lacked moral scruples and was incapable of making good choices, which made me feel embarrassed, ashamed, and humiliated. Never once was the fact that I was a child considered by anyone besides Mr. Gunn.

The way the prosecutor and judge described me in the courtroom was diametrically opposite to the way I felt on the inside. Here I sat, a bundle of terrified nerves, while I was being described as if I were a ruthless, fearless killer. Sometimes I would catch the words of the prosecutor or judge and wonder who they were talking about. It would take me a moment to realize it was me.

Mr. Gunn tried a little harder than Mr. Oblachinski to include me in the process, but he worked alone and didn't have time to explain everything that was happening or might happen, or what my choices were. He had a list of witnesses he wanted to put on the stand to testify on my behalf, including Dr. Lois Lee, founder of Children of the Night. Dr. Lee is the world's leading expert in rescuing child sex-trafficking victims. At that time, her organization had been in operation for fifteen years. (It's still going strong today.) This is how Mr. Gunn's request for her to testify at my trial was received by the DA:

Mr. Freer: "With regard to Dr. Lois Lee, it is my understanding that counsel's argument is that he basically wants her to come in and testify to the relationship that exists between a pimp and a prostitute."

The Court: "We have been calling that the—"

Mr. Freer: "Pimp/prostitute syndrome . . . In this particular case there are two problems with calling Dr. Lois Lee: One, is that there is no . . . authority that I know of to testify about this pimp and prostitute relationship that would have any bearing on the events of the early-morning hours of March 10. The other problem is that if she testifies that . . . there is a pimp/prostitute relationship or symbolic relationship that exists between the pimp and prostitute, how can she testify that even existed on March 9 or 10 because, obviously, it didn't exist. . . . So there is no relevance to testify, 'yes, there is a pimp/prostitute relationship' when in this particular case, the evidence presented so far shows that it was severed, if you will, on March 10. . . ."

Mr. Freer turned everything around and on its head in his legal arguments, which amounted to: GG is now dead; he couldn't still be my pimp.

Next, Mr. Gunn tried to call to the witness stand the psychiatrist who had examined me when I had tried to commit suicide after the gang rape. He wanted to show that I suffered from PTSD as a result of the rape and had long been in emotional turmoil because of GG's trafficking of me and the adult situations he had put me in from age thirteen. Mr. Freer objected that the rape was unrelated to the present case and that the doctor's testimony was irrelevant. The judge upheld Freer's objection.

Mr. Gunn also tried to call James Earl, but James Earl had

just been arrested for a murder and his lawyer advised him to plead the Fifth. James Earl and Johnny had already been questioned by detectives, who believed their false statements and concluded they were both peripheral to my case. Sergeant Detective Mark Boyer and Detective Ron San Filippo testified that James Earl had informed them that I had told him I shot GG because he wanted to put me out on the streets. James Earl said I had stolen GG's money and car of my own volition, and he was surprised I had given him some of the money. He said he didn't want someone like me around, so he had asked his sister to call the police and tell them where to find me. I now realize that this also explains why he left me alone at his house all day. He was hoping I would call my mom and tell her where I was.

James Earl also told the police that neither he nor Johnny had been anywhere near GG on the night of the crime. Of course they hadn't. They had set me up perfectly to take the fall.

The person who really disappointed me was Johnny. I thought he would stand up for me and tell the truth, but he echoed what James Earl said to the detectives and was never under suspicion. It slowly dawned on me that the look on his face when he got me to come outside was because he knew the cops were coming. What I still don't know is whether he was trying to protect me from them or deliver me to them.

In the end, I was the only witness the court and the DA permitted to testify on my behalf.

Mr. Gunn asked the court for permission to have my chains and shackles removed so as not to prejudice the jury. Everything that happened that day is a blur, but when I think back to when I took the stand, the judge may have denied even that. I don't recall the weight of chains around my waist, but I do recall the pulling of shackles around my ankles. I distinctly remember that the ten feet or so from the table where I was sitting with Mr. Gunn to the stand felt like a mile to walk, and the single step up to the witness stand, near the judge, felt like a flight of stairs. I sat on the wooden chair looking out over the courtroom. All the faces staring at me, except for my mother's and sister's, were male.

The judge asked Mr. Gunn if I had been sworn in, and he said I had not. The judge asked me to rise and raise my right hand. I was so nervous I had to pause to consider which hand was which. Then I had to tell myself to stand. I raised my right hand, and the clerk spoke: "Do you solemnly swear that testimony you may give in the matter now pending before this court will be the truth, the whole truth, and nothing but the truth, so help you God?"

I opened my mouth, but nothing came out until I cleared my throat. In a small voice I said, "I do," before sitting back down.

Anytime Mr. Gunn asked me questions designed to elicit information about my experience of trafficking, they were squelched by the DA or the judge, who asserted that they were irrelevant.

When Mr. Freer questioned me, he focused on the murder. He cross-examined me by asking the same questions over and over, in different ways. In the end, I was so confused, tired, and cranky that I just started answering *yes* to whatever he asked. The look in his eyes seemed to brook no dissent from me. He would later end his closing statement as follows:

Ladies and gentlemen, the defendant should be convicted of murder in the first degree. . . . And you know that if you find that the defendant committed murder that you are going to find the defendant used a firearm because, obviously, she did, she killed him with a firearm, she committed the act of murder with a firearm. And it's obvious, also, this murder was committed while she was intending to rob the victim, George Howard. And she was lying in wait, she was concealing her purpose, she did a surprise attack on the victim.

Gunn countered with his own remarks to the jury:

I think all of us could agree the worst thing that can happen is you make some decision and then you say a week later, or a month later, "I did the wrong thing." So, if you have a reasonable doubt about this case, your job, your duty in this case is . . . to return a verdict of not guilty. You know it is not easy. I am sure it is not easy as jurors, either, but it is not easy to sit here and defend someone who is seventeen years of age. Thank God it doesn't happen every day, it is not an easy task. And this is an adult place, this is an adult court, you are all adults. She suffers adult consequences at this point. If you have a question beyond a reasonable doubt that this is what happened, if you have a question, a serious question that the reason Sara Kruzan did this horrible thing—and again I agree with Mr. Freer, nobody is suggesting here that because of what Mr. Howard does, and no matter how reprehensible, underage girls [sic], nobody is saying he deserves to die because of that—but if she acted and killed him only because of the threats from James Earl Hampton, then she is not guilty of first degree murder. Again, I ask each of you to think about that, decide it in your own conscience so that you can come back and tell us individually, "This is what I know happened." I thank you all very much.

The jury was given its instructions and went off to deliberate. It took two days for word that a verdict had been reached. I was summoned back to the courtroom, shackled at the ankles and waist, and seated beside Mr. Gunn. I looked back and saw my mother, my sister, and a bunch of men in suits. The room was packed. I had a flash of hope: "This many people wouldn't show up if this wasn't going to be good news."

We all stood as the judge entered. Then we sat back down. The jury walked in, single file. The judge asked if they had reached a verdict. The foreman replied, "We have, Your Honor." He handed a paper to the clerk, who handed it to the judge.

Judge Hanks read the paper. I saw no reaction in his face as he handed it back to the clerk, who read the verdict aloud: "We, the Jury in the above-entitled action, find the defendant, Sara Jessimy Kruzan, intentionally killed the victim, George Howard, while lying in wait, within the meaning of Penal Code Section 190.2, subdivision (a), subsection (15). Dated May 11, 1995. Gary Ward, Foreperson."

There was a loud gasp and a wail from behind me. Mr. Gunn put his head down. "That means guilty," I thought, and allowed myself to float away.

As if from a distance, I heard Mr. Gunn ask the judge permission for my mom and sister to visit me at juvenile hall. The judge granted it with no argument.

I forced myself to return to my body. I felt tears rolling down my cheeks, but I wasn't aware of having begun to cry, and I didn't consciously understand what I was crying about. What I knew was that the trial had concluded badly.

The bailiff came to get me. I stood and looked back at my mom and sister and said to them, "It's okay. I'll be okay. I'm sorry."

I was escorted to the holding cell before being transported

back to juvenile hall. Soon my mom and sister visited me briefly. Mom was wailing as if it was she who had stood trial. Mya was quietly grieving. I wasn't crying anymore. I had made a decision in the van on the way back that I wasn't going to let my tears flow. It felt safer to keep the pain inside.

I was ordered to undergo intense psychological testing so that an informed decision as to my rehabilitative possibilities could be sent as a recommendation to the judge. My assessments were good. I was deemed capable of living a productive life with therapy. Nevertheless, Hang 'Em Hanks gave as good as his reputation. During the sentencing hearing a few months later, he handed down his judgment: life in prison without the possibility of parole, plus four years. Because of my age, my actual term in prison was not to begin until I reached twenty-five. Until then, I was to be held by the California Youth Authority.

7

It took me a while to fully understand the significance of the sentence of life without parole: It wasn't until some years later, when I was in the Chowchilla correctional facility, that I comprehended that it meant I was destined to live for the rest of my days in prison—plus four years after my death! It meant that I could never benefit from mercy. It meant that good behavior would count for nothing because there was nothing I could ever do to better my situation. At any age, let alone at seventeen, this concept would have been difficult to accept.

When I returned to juvenile hall from the sentencing hearing, I was put on suicide watch, as is customary for recipients of a sentence of either death or life without parole. I wasn't suicidal but in shock: confused, stunned, numb. And so I remained for a few weeks before I was transferred to the California Youth Authority (YA) facility in Ventura.

As I left juvenile hall, Ms. Graves hugged me and told me that she loved me and believed in me. She said, "We'll meet again, Sara. Until then, be strong and keep thinking positively."

Whereas the atmosphere at juvenile hall was a little like school, at YA a person under the age of twenty-five convicted of a serious crime actually begins serving their sentence. The YA's focus is to prepare those detained with life and vocational skills, ostensibly to be used after their release—not applicable, obviously, when your sentence allows for no possibility of parole. I was one of nine juvenile women at the YA who had been tried as adults. Once there, we were assigned minimum-wage jobs. Most of our earnings were appropriated. In my case, in addition to receiving my merciless sentence, I was ordered to pay a ten-thousand-dollar restitution fee to GG's family; 50 percent of any money I made going forward was to go toward that debt.

At YA I was assigned to work for TWA as a reservations agent. I underwent fifteen weeks of intensive training to learn how to use the computer system. The phone lines were linked to TWA's mainframe computer in Los Angeles. I was taught to enter codes identifying departure and destination cities, and I was expected to be courteous on the phone with customers. I enjoyed hearing the callers' different accents and allowing my imagination to take flight along with them, traveling the country and the world.

The corrections officers at YA treated us with a great deal less patience than those at juvenile hall. We were frequently reprimanded, yelled at, and put in isolation for negligible infractions. I didn't know it then, but I now realize that they were deliberately breaking us in for the prison experience we were headed toward. And I would soon discover that prison was unlike anything I'd experienced before. It was a world unto itself.

My sentence stipulated that I was to stay at YA until the age of twenty-five, when I would be deemed legally mature enough for adult prison, but this was not to be. A staff member at another California youth facility was murdered by a detainee. This led then governor Gray Davis to override the existing protocol and order all juvenile offenders in California

Youth Authority detention to be transferred immediately to adult prisons.

Barely eighteen, I found myself once again shackled, chained, and ushered onto a bus, this time headed for the Central California Women's Facility in Chowchilla, in the dead center of the state. Chowchilla, as it's commonly called, is the largest women's correctional facility in the United States. It is also the only female prison in California with a death row.

When we arrived, they brought us out of the van, unchained us, and led us into a large holding cell to await processing in the Receiving and Release building. One by one we had our photos taken and were interviewed by a staff member, who inquired about our particulars: birth dates, allergies, family members, religious faith. A female sergeant conducted the body search. She was an aggressive Latina who seemed very much to enjoy her authority. She didn't break any rules; the harshness of the search was standard in prisons. But there are people who are respectful and kind even though they have the power to humiliate you, and there are people who behave as she did.

She barked at us to strip. I was the youngest of the group and felt vulnerable and exposed, just as I had felt while being trafficked. She demanded that we spread our legs, wriggle our fingers, and raise our hands above our heads. If your breasts were big, you had to lift each with one hand to show that they hid nothing. She ordered us to wiggle our toes, spread our legs wider, and squat. "Open up those legs! Wider! Is that the best you can do? Wider! Now hold that position and cough. Cough again! Harder! Harder! Harder! Now spread your legs again. Squat and cough." Again we coughed in unison three times. Then she told us to turn around. Naked in that room, with so many eyes on me, I felt profoundly humiliated. Whenever I could, I would cross my hands over my breasts for some sense of decorum.

She made us turn again, "Now bend forward and spread yourself open so I can see." She had us grab our vagina area with our fingers and spread it as wide open as possible, then cough while doing that. The theory is that anything hidden inside would fall out because of loss of muscle control. After the cacophony of coughing subsided and nothing had dropped to the ground, the sergeant finally seemed satisfied.

Later, one of my cohorts confided that she had wrapped some rings and stuck them inside herself: "If that bitch had made me cough any harder, I swear they would have shot out and slapped her on her forehead."

You are not allowed to wear jewelry in prison without permission. Anything made of metal is considered a weapon. A ring, for instance, might be tied to a thread and used to hit somebody. Still people sneak jewelry in, along with other contraband. Sometimes they get away with it, but most often they don't.

We were handed rubber flip-flops we called "chanklas" and muumuus made from a rough, cheesecloth-like material printed with flowers, dots, or geometric patterns. They looked like old-lady house dresses. Each one was different, and they were all ugly. Then we were led across the A yard to be temporarily housed. We were put in cells on the top tier of a building, right in front of the corrections officers' station, so that the COs could keep a sharp eye on us during the adjustment period before we were assigned to one of the identical eight-person cells of a 256-bed block. We were to bunk up in pairs, but because our group was of an uneven number, even though I was the youngest, I was put in a cell by myself.

My new surroundings were mean in every way: cold, hard, and brutal. The prison smelled of rusted pipes. The round metal tables in the cafeteria—the "chow hall"—were industrial and unyielding, each bolted to the floor with small, evenly spaced stools rigidly attached to it by metal arms. The tables looked like satellites, or a den of spiders about to take off in an amusement ride of some sort, except they didn't move.

Nothing yielded to humanity. The round-toed, heavy, flat-soled, often mismatched shoes and clunky boots we were given to wear seemed designed to cause maximum discomfort. Our standard-issue clothing was blue pants made of a rough, heavy cotton blend that was supposed to resemble denim, and T-shirts with no pockets. We were provided with an allocation of institutional polyester underwear that was washed and bleached; nevertheless, some stains remained. We turned in our dirty underwear weekly, and the clean supply was redistributed with no allowance for size. You might wear a small and get size 3X panties, which you would then have to tie into knots to fit. Or you might normally wear a 3X and get a small, which you would have to cut the elastic from so that you could fashion some sort of thong covering. There was no softness anywhere. The towels, the mattresses, the grayish cotton sheets, the thin wool blankets, and even the toilet paper: all hard.

I was finally assigned to a cell and to C yard, where most of the LWOPs (prisoners sentenced to life without parole) were sent. My bunkies were a mix of races and ages. Nobody was rude or unwelcoming, but it always takes a while for incarcerated folk to warm up to someone new. People were constantly coming in and going out, transferring to different cells, leaving for court dates, being placed in solitary confinement for breaking a rule. Once you left your cell for any reason, there was no guarantee you would be returned to the same one.

Teresa was a tall, skinny Black woman in her late twenties with exquisite features and a loud laugh. Rosie was a grandmotherly Latina with black hair graying at the temples. Christina was a petite blonde in her mid-twenties. Tabby was in her thirties, stood about five foot three, and was maybe 230 pounds. Cindy was Tabby's younger sister, blond, blue-eyed, and quite a bit taller than Tabby at five foot seven. Nicc was a tall, bald Black woman. My bunkmates had all been inside for a while and had worked out a system of seniority in order to coexist harmoniously, including use of the bathroom. I had to take my place at the back of the line.

Inside our crowded cell was a lidless, porcelain toilet behind a door with rectangles cut out of it to limit privacy, two stainless-steel sinks, a little mirror on the wall, four sets of bunk beds, and eight high school–style lockers to hold all our possessions: letters, photos, two or three pairs of government-issued clothing, snacks bought from the canteen if you had any money, plus your soap, shampoo, toothpaste, toothbrush, and hairbrush. Every time I opened my locker, I couldn't help thinking, "If only I had kept my ass in school."

Mornings when I awoke, around 6 a.m., I was already hungry. My seven bunkies would also be up, bustling and getting ready for their various jobs and programs. As soon as the toilet was available, I would seize the opportunity. Usually, one of my cellmates would have just used it and the seat would still be warm. In such cramped quarters, proper hygiene was essential: you would always spray and wipe the toilet before sitting.

The first time I took a shower, I didn't know that I should hang a towel so that it would cover the bottom of the bathroom door, which was made of metal bars like a cage. I was oblivious to the fact that, from a particular angle in the dayroom on the floor below, everyone could look up and see your personal business through the bottom of the door. Some women I knew were downstairs playing cards, and one of them looked up and started yelling, "Sara, Sara, girl. I can see everything. Cover yourself."

I was given a job in the program office. So as not to be late, as soon as I heard "chow release," the announcement that food service was open, over the speakers, I'd rush from my room along with nearly two hundred other women in a cattle-like stampede to the chow hall. After breakfast I'd run back to my room to quickly brush my teeth, wash my face, grab my plastic coffee mug, and head to the program office in the yard. A corrections officer would unlock and open the gate to let me in. I would never know what to expect: whereas one officer might open the gate extra slowly out of hostility and dare you to say something about it, another might open it immediately and tell you to have a nice day. The prison system can be so relentlessly spirit crushing that a simple "good morning" can go a long way toward making you forget your circumstances for a moment.

At mealtimes, I would line up, then go sit with my tray at one of the spider tables. One day that first week, I was waiting for my food when an incarcerated woman, a table wiper, started flirting with me. I smiled politely but that was all. She kept at it, coming up to me at every meal. She would walk over to where I was sitting, her wet white rag in her hand. I didn't know what to do. She had seniority and was a big woman, about five foot ten and at least 210 pounds. I didn't want any trouble. Time and again she would say, "When you're finished, come over the wall so you can be my girl."

I had only just arrived at the prison, and the thought of women being intimate with each other had no appeal to me. It never occurred to me that, in time, it would come to feel natural to find romance and companionship among the women there.

I appealed to my friend Gina, who had been in the transfer van from YA with me, to help me out of my predicament.

"Next time we go to the chow hall and she tries to talk to me, I'm going to tell her I have a girlfriend. And you're going to be the girlfriend. Matter of fact, let's say we're married. Please, you gotta help me."

Gina, a gorgeous, petite, religious Latina who looked like a doll with long curly hair, agreed to help me out. Bless her heart, she knew how to be a friend.

When we were next in the chow hall, the woman approached me and smiled: "You been thinking about me, sweetie?"

"No." I pointed to Gina. "This is my girlfriend. I mean, this is my wife."

The woman looked at me as if I were full of it.

"That's your wife, huh? Let me see you kiss her."

Oh God. I had not thought this far ahead with the plan. Gina and I looked at each other. My eyes pleaded, "Please, Gina, kiss me. Please." We leaned toward each other and pecked at each other's lips.

With bravado, I said, "See?"

Gina, without thinking, automatically wiped her mouth clean with a sleeve before also saying to the woman, "See?"

It was clear that the woman found us less than convincing. "I know you all playing," she said.

I was thankful when she left me alone after that.

In Chowchilla, a multiplicity of types were jam-packed together. Some suffered from mental illness; some were seething with anger, which manifested itself in different ways, such as bullying or violence. To survive as a teenager among these adults, I had to be ever vigilant while relying on my instincts and reflexes. All the same, I made sure never to forget that everyone there was as traumatized as I was and, in some cases, more so.

In prison, of course, your every move is scrutinized. Choice is erased. Imagine contemplating the rest of your life knowing that you will never again have the opportunity to choose what to wear, what to eat, what to do, when to sleep, when to wake.

Two corrections officers worked each of the three 8-hour shifts overseeing our housing unit. The entire incarcerated population in California is subjected to a head count at 12:45 a.m., 2:45 a.m., 4:45 a.m., 12:00 p.m., 4 p.m., 9:15 p.m., and 11:30 p.m. Officers busy themselves confirming your individual California Department of Corrections (CDC) number, which you must recite when your name is called, except for the early-morning counts when they shine a flashlight into your cell to confirm you are in your bunk.

I both hated and liked being locked in at night. On the one hand, it was oppressive to feel trapped, but for the most part, I savored the hours of peace. That was when my imagination ran wild and my fantasies took flight, pondering things I wanted to do in life but knew I couldn't. I spent hours trying to come up with ways around the obstacles. One evening I had an amazing idea. I figured out how to execute it and announced to the room, "Guys, there's going to be a special event happening in here tonight after chow! Get your dancing socks ready!" I opened my locker. Powder: check! Socks: check!

I didn't even go down to chow; I stayed in the room to prepare. I had decided we would have a swing/skate dance party.

When everyone got back from dinner, I told them to put their socks on. I turned up the boom box, and dance music began to ring out in the room. I emptied a container of talcum powder onto the floor.

My six bunkmates (one bed was empty) were game. We all began skating and dancing around the room in our socks. Rosie was the strobe light operator. She switched the lights on and off to the rhythm of the music. The metal bunk beds helped us make turns in the small space with ease and grace. Before you knew it, we were gliding as if we were professional skaters at an Olympic-sized rink. We bumped into one another. We tried spins. Teresa's long limbs made her lose her balance, and she kept crashing into the beds. Nicc, who was naturally boisterous, was almost screaming. We added more powder to the floor and began to take solo turns, oblivious to anything but the present moment. Tabby had to sit down, she was laughing so hard, saying she was about to pee her pants. Next, we tied together two bedsheets at one end, then wrapped and looped them around the bunk-bed posts to make a hammock swing. We encouraged Tabby to get in, which was a bit of a feat. She was reluctant at first. As we all pushed her, I yelled, "Go, Tabby, go!" She disappeared into the hammock as if it were a cocoon, and we began to swing her back and forth.

The music was blasting. I was in seventh heaven "playing" with my friends. We were all having such a good time we forgot where we were. The next thing we knew, there was a loud banging on the door. It burst open and an angry middle-aged CO stood there and roared, "Turn that noise off!"

Our smiles melted. The light in our eyes went out, and in unison, our shoulders slumped.

Tabby tried to poke her head out from inside the sheet cocoon so that she could extricate herself, but the folds in the sheet prevented her. None of us went to help her. We just looked back and forth from the CO, who stood there glaring, to one another, to the mess in the room, wondering whether we should help Tabby. No one wanted to risk moving. We knew we were in trouble, and the question now was, how deeply in trouble were we? I sighed and spoke up. "I'm sorry. This was my idea. We were having a skate party."

The CO said, "You were too loud, and those sheets are now contraband because this is not what you're supposed to be doing with them. They should be on your beds. Knock it off and clean up this mess, or you'll be inviting me back."

We knew that would mean an in-depth search of the room,

and none of us liked those invasive inspections. If the room was a mess now, after a search, clothes and sheets would be tossed around and photos and letters would be strewn all over the place and sometimes torn.

The CO left the room and closed the door firmly to let us know he was unhappy with us. As he did so, the heaviness of his presence left the room as well. We had gotten away with no write-ups for our behavior. That was a positive.

Suddenly we heard a little voice: "Get me out of here!"

"Tabby!" We all rushed to help her, then turned the music back on, low. We wanted to continue playing, but all the air had been let out of our joy balloons, so we cleaned up in time to the music instead.

Moments of fun were sparse. As a troubled teen in an adult prison to whom psychiatric therapy was unavailable, I struggled to process the experience I was going through. Our inhumane treatment by the majority of the corrections officers, indeed by the penal system itself, served to reinforce the notion that we were horrible human beings beyond redemption, and therefore deserving to be put away for life. The argument constantly going through my head was "You're going to die here, so why bother to go to school?"

As the enormity of my predicament began to sink in during my first years at Chowchilla, I acted out. Sometimes I behaved obnoxiously. I would rebelliously talk back to a member of staff who asked me to be quiet or ordered me to hand back the rubber bands I'd used to cuff my pants at the bottom, harem-style, in an attempt to look cute. I racked up 115s and 128s, violation write-ups that go into your prison record, as if I were an avid stamp collector. Some transgressions add time to your sentence—in my case, that was a meaningless notion, so I could not have cared less. But then, ironically, as time passed, I slowly began to feel safe for the first time in my life. Being in prison always carries potential risk: a fellow incarcerated person might turn violent toward you; a guard might for no apparent reason become unconscionably abusive. And yet my days were organized, satisfying for the first time a deep-seated need I had harbored since childhood for structure. Curiously, through the regimented routine of prison life, I managed to develop a sense of security. That peace of mind led me to discover ways to develop an interest in myself and my future.

One day, I picked up a book in the dayroom, *Man's Search for Meaning*. Its author, the Holocaust survivor Viktor Frankl, was an Austrian psychiatrist and neurologist who spent several years in concentration camps, including Auschwitz. He wrote of "healing through meaning." The book chronicled his experience in the camps and stressed that focusing on a goal and a purpose can have a positive effect in a desperate situation. I took the book to my cell and read it three times. Each time, I saw something new and more profound in its pages.

Frankl uses the old-fashioned term "inmate," one that has become unpopular with those who have been, or still are, incarcerated, since it reduces one's identity to where one is, rather than who one is, in an already dehumanizing system. But Frankl's arguments do everything possible to restore a sense of humanity to the life of an incarcerated person. He outlines three reactions that a detainee (whether in prison or in a camp) will experience on some level: shock, apathy, and bitterness and depersonalization—the feeling of not being in your own body. Only the prisoner's spiritual self offers any saving grace. One must have hope for the future. If that hope is lost, one is condemned to permanent despair.

About a year and a half after arriving at Chowchilla, I received a curious piece of mail. We were allowed visitors on Thursday evenings, as well as weekends, and on that particular Thursday afternoon, the officer delivering mail came to my cell door, knocked, and called out, "Kruzan!" He dropped the letter on the floor and kicked it under the door. I picked it up and recognized Johnny's handwriting. Seeing it made me forget his betrayal. I carried the envelope to my bunk as if it were a treasure, opened it, and started to read.

"Sara, first off, I love you, I miss you, and I'm sorry. I wish what happened hadn't happened. . . ."

My eyes grew hot with tears. I grabbed the letter and held it to my heart. I had resumed reading it when the CO came by once more and said, "Kruzan, you have a visitor waiting by the name of Johnny Otis. As soon as the count clears, you can go see him." I couldn't believe the coincidence. Here I was, holding a letter from Johnny in my hand, even as he was here to see me.

I finished reading his letter. His opening sentence was the most memorable; the rest proceeded to describe the weather and songs he had heard on the radio.

I was so excited to see him, I didn't care how I looked. After slapping some water on the flyaway bits, I pulled my hair into a ponytail and put on a blue state-issued sweatshirt and jeans. This was as presentable as I was going to be. As soon as the count was done, I left the cell, went out to the yard, and walked as fast as I could, without giving the appearance of running, to the visiting area. The five-minute walk dragged. I stripped for the guards, was cleared, and got dressed again. I opened the heavy metal door and stepped into the room. I paused at the security station to get my table assignment. I searched the faces there. Right away I saw Johnny standing at the vending machine. My heart pounded. As I walked toward our table, he turned and spotted me. He looked exactly as he had the last time I had seen him, standing in front of James Earl's house the day I was arrested.

"I got your favorites," he said, gesturing to a pint of straw-berries and a bottle of Snapple he had bought from the machine.

His long arms enveloped me, and I fell into them as if we had never been separated.

We were only nineteen, but to me it felt as though we had been alive for much longer. He said he still wanted to marry me and would wait for me.

We held hands, ate strawberries, and talked about this and that—every inconsequential thing but the crime.

Finally, he took both my hands, looked into my eyes, and said, "I am sorry I didn't protect you."

We both slid into an awkward silence. The reality of him saying this now hit me like a gut punch. I gently explained that, with my LWOP sentence, I would never be leaving prison.

I said, "You're young. Go to school, get a job, have a family."

He had tears in his eyes. "You have strawberries stuck be-tween your teeth."

We both laughed, and for a moment everything seemed okay again. He felt like home to me. For a second I thought, "Maybe he and I can figure out a way to make this work." As I tried to imagine how we might sustain a relationship, the CO announced that visiting hours were over.

Johnny and I lingered at the table as if, now that we had reconnected, we didn't want to be apart again. We were the last to say good-bye. Public displays of affection had to be kept to the barest minimum. We hugged quickly. I stood and watched as he disappeared from the room.

I went back to my cell with rekindled hope. I was not alone in the world, I thought. Johnny loved me and wanted to be with me. How else to explain this miracle, the coincidence of my receipt of his letter and his visit? Johnny and I exchanged lighthearted letters over the next few months. We wrote about TV shows and songs we liked and declared how much we missed each other. As he didn't visit me again, I told myself he was probably too busy looking for a job or working to provide for us in anticipation of our marriage.

About five months after Johnny's visit, on Thanksgiving Day, I was at the chow hall eating dinner. A woman who lived in my housing unit approached me and said that every time she saw me she was stunned by how much I looked like her daughter. She had photos to show me. Sure enough, her daughter and I did resemble each other. We could have been sisters. There was a photo of her daughter, pregnant, cutting a wedding cake. I said, "Congratulations!" as I turned to the next one in the pile. It was of the newlyweds. When I saw the groom's face, I had never been so taken by surprise in my life.

"Please tell me his name is not Johnny Ray Otis Jr.," I said to the woman.

With a proud grin she said, "Yes. He's my son-in-law!"

I blinked back shocked tears and could not speak. I continued to stare at the photographs as I tried to think of something to say. That Johnny was married and about to become a father was upsetting enough; even more so was that he had failed to mention any of this when he had visited and in our letters. I shuffled the deck of photos, not looking down at them anymore.

I gave them back to her and blurted, "You don't know about me?"

She looked puzzled and said, "No."

I said, "I'm Sara Kruzan. Johnny was my boyfriend."

"Oh my gawd, I have heard about you!"

"Close custody recall" sounded over the loudspeaker, giving me an excuse to say a quick goodbye before heading to be locked into my cell for the night.

I wrote to Johnny, expressing my disappointment at yet another betrayal by him. He did not write back.

A few months later, on a whim, I telephoned his mom's house, and she accepted my collect call. I told her what had happened. She said that Johnny was depressed, and she didn't want to upset him by telling him I had called. There was nothing much to say after that.

At least three more months went by before a bright yellow envelope from Johnny Ray Otis Sr. was delivered to my cell one evening. I had never met Johnny Ray Otis Sr. Compared to his son's, his cursive handwriting was exceptionally neat. I ripped open the envelope and read:

Dear Sara,
    First I apologize for my son's behavior. Though I wasn't around physically much I didn't raise him to do what he has done to you. He told me everything.
    Being I was incarcerated and understand loyalty I'd like to step in and hold that space for you. You need anything? I've enclosed $20.00 for your commissary as well. Again, I apologize and hold your head up.
    With respect,
    Johnny Sr.

Years later I heard that Johnny Jr. worked as a truck driver, had two or three sons whom he adored, and had become a heavy drinker.

It took me two years to get over Johnny this second time around, during which I began a relationship with a woman who was one of my bunkies. I'll call her "H." She was scheduled to go to ad seg (administrative segregation) while being investigated for some infraction or other; I don't remember exactly what. Ad seg meant you were removed from the general population and put in solitary confinement. If you were found guilty of whatever they were investigating, you were sentenced to time in the SHU (security housing unit). H had gathered up her things and left them out on her bunk to take with her. She had access to my locker and had included some of my clothes and my hairbrush with her pile.

I was working at the PIA dental lab. (The Prison Industry Authority sells or offers prison-manufactured goods or services to public entities.) There, I had been trained to make full and partial dentures for prisoners in the state of California. I liked the job, though my earnings in prison took a big hit compared to my YA pay, which conformed to the national minimum wage. In prison, I was paid forty-five cents an hour for seven and a half hours a day, minus the deduction going toward my restitution debt.

Someone came by and said, "Hey, Sara, H is going to go to jail [which is what we called ad seg], and she's in the cell packing up some of your clothes and papers."

I was able to get a pass to leave so that I could see what was happening. When I got to the room, I saw my stuff included with hers.

Another bunkie told me, "They're bringing her here under escort right now."

Furious, I set out to meet her. I marched from the housing unit back out to the yard. I saw her and the escort CO walking from a distance. The CO was yelling, "ESCORT, stand down!" meaning everyone had to stop what they were doing and stand still as the officer and prisoner passed.

I disobeyed the order. I kept walking toward them, yelling, "You can't do what you think you're doing, H. You can't just take my stuff."

Soon I was in front of her and the officer. I faced H. Though she held her hands behind her back, H was not cuffed. She broke away from the officer, got up close and personal, and said, "What the fuck are you going to do about it, bitch?"

I pounced on her and we began fighting hard. In that moment H was every person who had ever hurt me—I didn't care about the consequences of pummeling her. The prison alarm went off. COs started running toward us from all directions. The female CO who had been escorting H and trying to break up the fight firmly ordered me to "sit down now!"

Her voice breached my fury. I froze, then sat on the ground. So did H.

The CO said, "You hit me, Kruzan. I know it was not intentional, but I have to write you up."

I nodded. I was still seeing red. I wanted to cry but didn't want H to see how embarrassed and hurt I was feeling. The CO's accusation seemed fair to me. I had hit her while trying to get to H.

That night, I myself was sent to ad seg pending an investigation. I was placed in solitary confinement for a month. The incident report concluded that I had assaulted staff, even though the CO had confirmed that my transgression was accidental. Higher-ups disagreed, and I was ordered to spend a ten-month SHU term at Valley State Prison, which was across the street from Chowchilla. The VSP SHU accepted overflow.

Although VSP was so close, I was transported there by bus in a cage. I walked into the VSP SHU building feeling defeated. I had come into contact with the omnipotence of the system. I felt like giving up because I realized I couldn't fight it. As I was escorted down the tier, I heard women shouting, yelling, crying, screaming unintelligible words.

My cell was eight by ten feet. There were slabs of cement on either side of the windowless room, a toilet, and a tiny sink. It was cold. The recycled air smelled thick and awful. Not long after landing there, I understood the screams and cries I had heard when I arrived. Spending so much time alone in a small space like that can break a person.

You'd get a couple of hours of yard time on Tuesday and another couple on Friday. Once I witnessed a brutal fight between prisoners. The staff started spraying rubber bullets and I ducked in fear. I never went outside again during my stint there. My only foray out of the cell was for the permitted two showers a week.

I repeated my mantra, "You're going to get through this, Sara." Still, I could feel that I was beginning to lose myself.

Three months into my SHU term, I began communicating through the vent with my next-door neighbor, a gregarious red-haired woman named Sandy, who was a few years older than me. She had been in the SHU a year already. Soon, because of good behavior, she was allowed to transfer to my cell. She slept on one cement slab, and I on the other. It was a blessing to be in the company of another person, to talk to and laugh with someone. Sandy had a cassette player, and she and I exercised to the Destiny's Child song "Survivor." I credit that song and Sandy with helping me get through the SHU.

After eight and a half months, I was released for good behavior. I said good-bye to Sandy, was chained up, shackled, stuck in a mesh cage, put on a bus with a lot of other cages, and transported back to Chowchilla, across the street. The officers on the bus carried semi-automatic weapons. I wondered, "Why are y'all armed that way for me? Do you really think I am that dangerous?"

When I got back to C yard, Nicc, Tabby, and Gina brought me new pants and made sure I had fresh sheets. They looked out for me and helped me try to settle back into the cell. They knew something I didn't. Later that day, when I went to the chow hall, I knew something in me had changed. The sound of women eating, talking, and laughing assaulted my senses. I was overcome with a feeling of anxiety, panic, and fear. Lack of sun and fresh air and the long period of isolation had done a number on me. I didn't understand why my physical and emotional responses were betraying me like this. I started spiraling right there in the chow hall. I dumped my tray without eating anything and walked outside, where I paced back and forth and breathed deeply in and out until I felt a bit calmer. Then I turkey-trotted—because of course you can't run on the premises for fear of getting shot by one of the guards up in the gun towers—back to my housing unit. I was terrified that if I did something wrong, I might get into trouble again and receive another write-up. I didn't think I could survive being sent to the SHU again.

One day, without explanation, I was summoned to a meeting with a high-ranking official at Chowchilla. Lieutenant Cooper was a middle-aged Black woman on the verge of retiring after working for decades in the prison system. She had seen it all and was considered tough but fair. She worked in the watch-tower, oversaw the evening shift, and made sure the facility ran smoothly. She had been reviewing files and came across mine. When I got to her office, she motioned for me to come in and sit down.

"Guess what? You and I have the same birthday, January eighth," she said.

I could not believe my ears. She laughed at the surprised look on my face.

"I've been looking at your file," she continued. "You are so young, Sara, a baby. But look at your record." (Those were the days when I was quick to mouth off and had collected more than my share of 115s and 128s.)

I might have shrugged. I know I did inwardly.

"Look, I know why you're here. I know your sentence, and how impossible it is to have hope. But you have to try to not let this environment take away from who you are and what you believe in. I've been watching you. You're an intelligent young lady, and I want you to try to live up to your potential."

I was stunned that someone like her had noticed me and was taking the time to speak to me as if I mattered to her. I told her I felt hopeless and defeated. She nodded and said, "I know, but you can't let yourself feel that way. What if the laws change someday? What if people who write the laws realize they shouldn't give children sentences like yours? What if new laws are applied retroactively? Anything is possible. If the laws change, you need to live right so that your record reflects that." For whatever reason, what she said reached me that day. I heard her. She relit my sense of possibility. She empowered me not to give up.

It helped that I was tired of being angry. As I began to get over my bitterness at my sentence, I signed up for classes and reapplied myself to studying. I managed to earn an AA degree in social and behavioral science from Feather River College, which sent instructors to the prison to teach us. I enrolled in courses for anger management and self-esteem building and participated in an Alternatives to Violence workshop. This taught us to distinguish among various forms of violence and how best to respond to them. Much of the content was common sense, for example, no man should ever put his hands on a woman unless the context is consensual, but it was surprising how many people were unaware of how to identify these actions in others. I learned that even silence can be a form of violence. I began to teach hip-hop dancing classes for my block mates and other women in my housing unit. Eventually, I worked myself up to the honor dorm. To earn a place there you must be free of disciplinary infractions for an extended period. The honor dorm comes with certain privileges: being first in line for chow, and more lenient visitation rights.

At Chowchilla, I discovered my love of painting by participating in the annual contest to paint the walls of the dayrooms. The unit would throw out ideas for the theme—an emotion such as love, for example, or a particular color—and a committee of us volunteers would vote on them. One year the theme was Starbucks. We painted the sign, the entrance, and decorated the room and walls to look like an outdoor café. We made cardboard people and painted lit-up Christmas trees and tables with steaming cups of coffee. On decision day, the warden went from dayroom to dayroom, judging our art and choosing a winner. Cake and ice cream were the prize. My team won several years in a row.

Painting helped me to release not only my anger at my circumstances but also the happiness inside me. I painted to brighten our environment, to make it more interesting and joyful. I told myself that, with a stroke of a brush, I could neutralize all the times GG, Roosevelt, and hundreds of Johns had assaulted me, and that my painting might also help to alleviate the pain suffered by my mates.

When I was younger and ran track, I found that if I focused on my feet hitting the ground as I moved my legs, it was easier not to get out of breath. I kept telling myself that the burn felt good, that I needed to feel it to reach my goal. I believe that in prison, I somehow figured out how to transform the physical mechanics of running into the spiritual mechanics of surviving by living day to day with fortitude. The process of coming into my own was slow and sometimes painful, but ultimately enriching. Prison taught me everything good that I know today about patience, perseverance, love, and friendship.

With my bunkies, I was mindful of the near miss we'd had, punishment-wise, the night we skated in the room, so I came up with quieter ways we could enjoy ourselves. Sometimes I'd say, "Let's go to the beach." We would each spread out on our thin, frayed government-issue towels and pretend they were luxurious, plush beach blankets. All of us—me, Tabby, Nicc, Rosie, and the others—donned pretend sunglasses, turned off the lights, closed our eyes, and listened to the ocean in our daydreams.

One evening, Tabby and I were sitting on bunk beds in our cell watching a TV talk show. It might have been Sally Jessy Raphael, Geraldo Rivera, or Oprah. The guests were a couple of lawyers talking about their pro bono cases. I heard one say, "I'm not going to stop until I get this kid out."

I turned to Tabby and said, "One day a lawyer's going to come in here and hear my case and say they're going to get me out."

Tabby said, "Yeah, right. Neither you nor I are ever going home."

Both of us had been sentenced to life without parole. We women rarely discussed the particulars of our cases with one another, but we usually knew what someone's sentence was. Tabby and I were aware that our chances of freedom were all but impossible.

But I reiterated, "No, I'm going home," and I suddenly realized that I believed what I had just said with all my heart. As uncanny as it might sound, the lawyer's passion on the show fired me up with hope that there might be someone out there willing to fight relentlessly on my behalf.

8

In 2004, nine years into my sentence, I showed up for my annual meeting with my counselor, Mr. Garrett. In prison, you meet with your assigned counselor once a year or so to go over your prison record. The counselor is also usually up to date on any changes in the law and can offer advice about new opportunities for appeal or legal strategies to improve your situation. None was ever applicable to me. When I was first assigned to Mr. Garrett, I was apprehensive. He was a Black man, and given my recent history, I was not comfortable with any man, Black or white. In time, however, I grew to like and trust him. He seemed genuinely to care about me and was constantly searching for overlooked loopholes in my case or legal revisions that might affect me.

As we went over my case this time, Mr. Garrett asked me what had happened to James Earl Hampton. He felt that my trial had been particularly unfair given James Earl's prior convictions. As he pursued this line of thought and questioned me about how I felt I had been represented, I was conflicted. Street code demands that you refrain from getting anyone else in trouble. I had implicated James Earl in the murder of GG, and the police had ignored me. And because I had told Johnny about GG and how much cash he carried on him, I felt

I was also partially responsible for what had happened. Still, Mr. Garrett considered my sentence an outrage and was very disappointed that he could see no way around it.

"Let's see what James Earl Hampton has been up to," he said. As I sat in front of him, he searched online and found out that James Earl was now serving a life sentence for an exceptionally brutal crime. He had raped and killed a woman in front of her children, after ransacking her house and demanding money. I left the meeting with Mr. Garrett pondering the fact that James Earl and I had ended up in the same place, so to speak, serving life sentences for murder.

The violence-prevention and self-esteem-building programs I attended during my incarceration often invoked restorative justice, a concept that stresses the open engagement between perpetrator and victim, with the goal of conflict resolution. The U.S. parole system is based on a prisoner's willingness to assume responsibility for his or her crime. In the programs I participated in, we were encouraged to come to terms with our actions and their consequences. It is an ongoing process to accept that you can never completely erase your offense, however ardently you wish you could. I cried for GG's mother, who lost a son because of me. I cried for my own mother, who lost a daughter. I cried for myself, and for James Earl and Johnny. I continue to mourn the roles we all played on the night of GG's murder.

Unless you have special dispensation from the warden, there are complicated rules governing communication between prisoners. Incarcerated people may not receive mail from another incarcerated person or from someone who has been free for less than a year. One morning, not long after my meeting with Mr. Garrett, I decided to write to James Earl. I knew the rules, but my desire to write to him was so overpowering that I didn't think of them that day. Given the conditions, it seems a miracle that my letter to James Earl reached him and that his response, a year or so later, reached me.

Learning that James Earl and I were serving the same sentence made me feel a little differently toward him. I bore a lot of guilt for having shot and killed GG, and I wondered whether James Earl felt this way too. I had pulled the trigger, and I could have chosen not to do so. I could not ignore my accountability. In the years since it had happened, I had given much thought to the crime I had committed. I had come to terms with the factors that caused me to follow through with James Earl's order.

My letter to James Earl was formal but pleasant. I wanted him to know that I was not harboring feelings of hatred or blame toward him. In fact, I was releasing him from any culpability regarding my case. I wished that in response he would explain why he hadn't told the truth when I was arrested, but I did not expect him to, and was reconciled to that. I folded the letter and put it in an envelope. I didn't seal it, because in prison, all letters must be read and checked before they can go out. I said to myself, "You don't have to worry about James Earl anymore. Whether or not he answers, you have acknowledged and forgiven him respectfully." I dropped off the envelope and went about my day. I was looking forward to a date I had with my friends to play dominoes in the game room.

I sat with the usual group, Nicc, TBird, Chubby, Capone, Kerstin, and Shawty, on bolted-down plastic chairs at one of the square tables. As we started the game, we realized we didn't have any paper to keep score. I went to the bulletin board and snatched off a flyer so as to use the back of it, and started shuffling dominoes. We had a good time and laughed a lot, though each of us was intensely competitive. Everyone was playing to win. The victor—usually one of the reigning champions, TBird or Nicc—would shout, "Domino, muthafuckas!" On this day Nicc won fair and square. As we stood up to leave, I noticed there was still space on the back of the flyer to keep score of another game, so I took it back to my cell.

A few weeks later, I was sorting through the junk in my cubby and found the folded piece of paper. I picked it up and flattened it out. I saw that it was a notice from Human Rights Watch advising anyone who had received a sentence of life without parole as a juvenile to contact them. I could not get a pen into my hand fast enough to write a short letter giving my name, age when incarcerated, and the reason for my sentence. True, I had followed similar leads before, writing to prisoner rights advocacy groups and pro bono lawyers featured in newspapers or on television, to little avail and much discouragement. But each time I reached out, I felt a whisper of possibility.

About six months later, I received an envelope back from Human Rights Watch containing a simple questionnaire asking for basic information: name, background, race, and so forth. I mailed in my responses and, again, waited. In prison, you learn to wait in a particular manner. You have hope, but you also understand that you must tamp down positive expectations. And you do it all with an enormous amount of patience.

While waiting to hear back from Human Rights Watch, I received a reply to my letter from James Earl. He let me know that he was now a Muslim, had done a lot of soul searching, and had changed. He said that he had come to realize how ungodly his way of life had been. He acknowledged that he had made some terrible mistakes and asked me to forgive him because he knew that, as a child, I had been unable to make mature decisions for myself. He said he was sorry and that I did not deserve what had happened to me.

There are no words to describe the feeling that washed over me upon reading James Earl's letter. It was an epiphany that allowed me to begin to forgive myself for taking GG's life. For years, I had held James Earl largely responsible for my fate. But now, as I read his words, any residual bitterness I felt toward him dissolved.

James Earl also declared that he would write letters attesting to the truth of his involvement in GG's murder. These letters of support, which he wrote over a period of months, were included in my file presented a few years later to the court. As well as the boost they may have given my case, I like to think they might also go some way toward repairing his own reputation in the eyes of the system.

Another six months had gone by with no response to my completed Human Rights Watch questionnaire. Then, one April morning, a CO announced that a visitor was waiting to see me. As I walked through the yard, I heard "ESCORT!" booming over the loudspeaker, indicating that we should all stand still. Two officers in full protective gear were walking a woman incarcerated on death row across the yard. She had on waist chains of the kind I had also worn in the past, so instead of staring, out of respect for her, I just looked up at the sky. It could very easily have been me. Most of us lifers had a "there but for the grace of God go I" attitude toward those on death row.

I took a deep breath and walked through the heavy metal doors toward the visiting rooms. I glanced to my left and saw a woman with salt-and-pepper hair sitting at a table in an area reserved for meetings with lawyers. I sat down across from her; she looked me in the eye, leaned across the table, introduced herself, and firmly shook my hand. Pat Arthur was an attorney with the National Center for Youth Law.

Pat and I talked for hours that day—about my life before

prison, my trial, my incarceration so far. More than once she reached over, squeezed my forearm, and said: "You just keep up the good fight." The spark in her eye encouraged me. At one point, she got up to buy snacks from the vending machine, and I noticed that she used a cane for balance as she walked. I jumped up to try to help her, but she brushed me aside with the cane—she was there to help, not to be helped. Later she explained that a tumor was growing in her spine, slowly paralyzing her. I was in awe of Pat's feistiness and fierce independence. As I spent more time with her, I came to learn that she considered her cases to be the most important thing in her life. Pat is someone who lets nothing get in the way of her passionate desire to see justice done and wrongs corrected.

Pat went back to the free world, and I went back to my caged life until about a year later, when I got word that a camera crew from Human Rights Watch would visit to film an interview with me. On the day of the interview, I tried to look my best. I parted my hair on the side and styled it as well as I could. I had on a pair of approved earrings, and I wore a prison-issued navy sweatshirt over a white T-shirt.

I had spent the morning at my job stretching U.S. star field flags for the state of California. I enjoyed working in prison, not just because it provided me with a little pocket money to purchase snacks at the canteen, but also because I felt as if, by sending something out beyond the prison walls, by working on these flags that were destined to fly outside, a part of me was venturing beyond the walls too.

Stretching a flag is not as easy as it sounds. They come in different sizes—three by five, five by eight, four by ten, eight by twelve—and they're made from different materials: cotton, or cotton and nylon. You place the flag on top of a big, wide table and stretch it by rubbing and pulling at the material until the stripes are absolutely straight, and then secure it with a staple gun. The fabrics we worked with were the cheapest possible, and they were rough to the touch. My knuckles would become worn from rubbing, so I'd have to wrap them with tape to prevent drops of blood from dripping onto the cloth. If that happened, I would not be paid for the flag. A CO having a bad day might also give a 115 for messing it up. Any flaws in my work would result in a deduction from my pay and, given that I owed ten thousand dollars to his family for the murder of GG, every cent counted.

I had advanced to become a leader at work, supervising a crew of twelve. That day, I was able to leave early because I had a "ducat." In the Middle Ages, a ducat was a gold coin. In prison, it is a white or yellow paper pass permitting you movement within the institution. You are required to show a ducat to go to a medical appointment or to attend a legal visit or a meeting with your counselor. I kept checking the clock and finally left the work area, allowing myself time to turn in my tools and clear the metal detector before heading to the visiting rooms.

Pat Arthur was waiting for me, along with Allison Parker and a cameraman. Allison was a young lawyer with brown hair, a gentle expression, and kind eyes. She was wearing coral-colored lipstick and, like Pat, gave me the impression that she cared about what I had to say by looking me in the eye and giving me a break when I became overwhelmed by her questions, which was often. It was not easy to speak about my childhood and how I met GG. Rather than interacting with the cameraman, I directed my attention to Allison, who was conducting the interview. Like Pat, she spoke to me, not at me, and didn't avert her eyes. (You'd be surprised how many people coming in from outside look away when speaking to an incarcerated person.)

I was nervous, and focused intensely on Allison. She asked me to talk about GG and how he had groomed me. As I began to describe the first time he had sex with me at age thirteen, shame washed over me. I stared down at my jeans and the white socks I was wearing with my black-and-white tennis shoes. I felt embarrassed recounting the details, trying not to sound vulgar. These compassionate women moved me: they were intently listening to me speak forthrightly about my life, who I was, and what I had done—about the child, the prostitute, the murderer, and the "inmate": CDCR #W59700.

When they finished asking questions and the camera operator stopped recording, I broke down. The man left the room, and the two women joined me for a good cry. Each hugged me tightly. As I watched them leave and heard the thud of the heavy door closing behind them, I felt lighter. I had never had the opportunity to tell my story as I had to Pat and Allison that day. It was profoundly cathartic.

A few weeks later, Pat returned for an attorney-client visit and somehow managed to get permission to bring in her laptop. She played me the video we had made. Watching it, I felt a welter of emotions: embarrassment, humiliation, fear, sadness, shyness, amazement, and pride. Pat explained that, after it had been sent the country over to lawyers and policy makers concerned with juveniles sentenced to life in prison, it would be uploaded—whatever that meant—on the internet to You-Tube, where thousands would see it, including some who may have shared aspects of my experience. I was clueless about the impact the video might have, as I knew nothing about the internet, which had come into its own during the years I had been incarcerated, nor did I know what YouTube was. All the same, Pat seemed excited, and her excitement was infectious.

As the guard unlocked the yard gate, allowing me back into the housing unit, I looked at him and he looked at me, maybe a bit longer than was comfortable. I wanted him to know that I saw him and, more important, that I needed him to see me.

Watching the video had given me hope, and I wanted him
to witness the hope I was feeling, not only for myself but for
everyone else there too. He smiled softly and stepped aside in a
gallant manner. I sensed him honoring my feelings and giving
me respect as I stepped forward into the yard.

Even the ground beneath my feet felt different. The yard
looked inviting and fertile instead of desolate and dry. Knowing that my truth and my story had been recorded forever, and
that people would see it, ignited my faith in the possibility that
my circumstances might change. For the next seven years, Pat
Arthur visited me once a month. Throughout that time, she
strategized pathways to my release with partners at the law firm
with which she was associated.

The video was shared among California politicians to raise
awareness of the dangers facing children in certain commu-
nities. People began reaching out to me. Among them was
Carrie Christie, a mother of two, and her best friend, Susan
Burger, both students at San Diego State University (SDSU).
In their first letter, they declared that they had watched the
video and were inspired to do something to help me. They
were both executive board members of the San Diego Dem-
ocratic Women's Club and passionate about women's issues.
They were determined to start "good trouble" to free me. Letters from Carrie continued to arrive almost daily. Her friendli-
ness, enthusiasm, and fierce will leaped off the page. She always
wrote as if we had known each other all our lives. Her correspondence, filled with news of her life and the world outside, became the highlight of my days. My bunkies, too, would
eagerly listen as I read her letters aloud. Carrie was indefati-
gable, her seriousness of purpose steely.

Within two years, she had started a movement that rippled
around the world. Carrie launched Free Sara Kruzan, a cam-

paign for my release, relying on marketing and advertising tactics to galvanize public attention. She harnessed political, educational, religious, and community organizations as forums to discuss my case and garner support. Senator Leland Yee, a Democrat from California, posted my video on his website. Next, Carrie targeted influential men and women, from politicians to Hollywood actors, and staged "community conversation" events to discuss my plight. These featured celebrities who had seen the video, including Demi Moore, Ashton Kutcher, Mira Sorvino, and Jada Pinkett Smith, drawing big crowds.

For the "community conversations," Carrie blew up and juxtaposed photos of me as a child with me as an incarcerated person in my prison uniform. When her daughter, Madison, outgrew a pair of black patent-leather dress shoes and Carrie was about to donate them to charity, it occurred to her that Madison was around the age I had been when GG first targeted me. Carrie believed that, for people attending the events, seeing a child's black patent-leather shoes with a button strap would be a powerful symbol of my innocence and youth at the age when I was first groomed. The shoes traveled all over California with Carrie as she went from event to event.

One day, Carrie asked me what my favorite colors were, and I told her pink and yellow. She wanted to know why. "Yellow reminds me of summer and warmth and sunflowers," I said. "Pink reminds me of love and connection. They're good colors, representing good things." She brought pink and yellow roses and a huge poster of me framed in yellow and pink to the California State Capitol in Sacramento, and to a candlelight vigil she organized to protest my incarceration and demand my release.

By early 2012, it seemed as if the six years of legal maneuvering by Pat Arthur and her team, and the resourcefulness of Carrie and her fellow activists and supporters, had started to pay off. As part of the Free Sara Kruzan campaign, Carrie began an online Change.org petition and posted it on Facebook and Twitter. A Facebook page under the same name featured news stories, celebrity endorsements, and crowdsourced initiatives, in addition to photographs of people the world over—in Nigeria, New Zealand, Zambia, Hungary, Italy, Denmark, Romania, and Saudi Arabia—holding signs that said FREE SARA KRUZAN and I AM SJK. Carrie would print out the photos and comments posted each week and mail them to me. The digitalization of the support and its far-reaching effect baffled me at first; I didn't know what to make of it. The petition and the campaign were meant to bolster a legal appeal to California's then governor, Arnold Schwarzenegger, to grant me a pardon based on the circumstances of my life at the time I killed GG. But since the laws that had condemned me were still on the books, how could I hope for that?

The day Carrie printed out the entire Change.org petition and took the quarter of a million signatures to the Riverside District Attorney Paul Zellerbach's office, she brought along a hot pink, spray-painted folding chair and placed it across the street from the government building, signifying that she was saving a seat for me when I was home and free. People gathered around it holding signs saying I AM SARA and FREE SARA. Carrie marched over to the offices and demanded to deliver the petition in person. When she finally got past the reluctant security guards, she handed it over to the DA's spokesperson saying, "This is not justice. This is a community outcry. Let's fix it."

On January 2, 2012, Governor Schwarzenegger did not pardon me but instead commuted my sentence from life without parole to twenty-five years to life. This was huge: I would now have an opportunity to face a parole board, which would decide whether I might be granted my freedom after I had served a minimum of twenty-five years.

In June 2012, my lawyers were successful in getting the California Supreme Court to order a hearing in the Riverside County Superior Court to determine whether I should be allowed a new trial so that they could argue that an "intimate battered partner defense" should have been presented at my trial. The "intimate battered partner defense" is an offshoot of what used to be called "battered woman syndrome," a term coined by the psychologist Lenore Walker in the 1970s. The defense allows women convicted of killing an abuser with whom they had a sexual, romantic, or cohabitational relationship to file a writ of habeas corpus with evidence demonstrating how the battering and its effects led to the killing. My lawyers' argument was that, if expert testimony relating to intimate partner battering and its effects had been received in evidence at the trial that landed me in prison for life, the result of the proceedings might have been very different. Judge Hanks's refusal to admit this line of defense disallowed connecting the murder to my relationship with GG, which affected my right to a fair trial.

Soon after the hearing was ordered, Carrie told me about One Billion Rising, a global campaign that the playwright and activist Eve Ensler, creator of *The Vagina Monologues,* had announced to end rape and sexual violence against women. Carrie explained that One Billion Rising was "a call for one billion women and all the men who love them to walk out of their jobs, schools, offices, homes on February 14, 2013, and strike, rise and dance . . . a global action to be determined and carried out locally. Every city, town, village, and person would determine what they were rising for—to end FGM, to remember their daughter's rape, to stop sex slavery, to educate young boys and girls about non-violent sexual relations." Carrie asked me to mobilize the women in building #512 (my cell block) to join the protest at a particular time, so as to contribute to the healing energy of the worldwide initiative. She explained that our actions did not have to be captured on camera; it was the collective intention of women gathering together at the same time across the globe that mattered.

Our circumstances, however, clearly posed certain challenges. I told her, "I'm not sure if we can 'rise' in solidarity at four-thirty p.m. That's count time." I didn't know how I could possibly align everybody without running afoul of CDCR rules and the prison authorities. We laughed at the ambitiousness of her invitation and the obstacles I would have to overcome to achieve her goal.

But I was game. I took it upon myself to approach Ms. Paine. Ms. Paine and Ms. Wait were white corrections officers assigned to my building who happened to be sisters. Ms. Paine was around five foot eight and skinny. She wore her brown hair in a ponytail and always had on a crisp, clean uniform. Ms. Wait was a little chubbier, with a few more wrinkles. Her blue eyes twinkled when she laughed. Ms. Paine's eyes were brown, and she was more serious, even though she was the younger sibling. They had both worked at the prison for years and were close to retirement. I said, "Ms. Paine, a lot of the ladies in building 512 would like to participate in One Billion Rising. Could you count us before four-thirty, send the count to control, then let us join the movement early before the whole state clears?"

She tightened her lips, looked at me, inhaled and exhaled audibly, thought about it, and said okay.

I couldn't believe it! I ran up to my housing unit and said, "People, we're doing it!"

We quickly cut out little paper circles to represent the world.

I passed them out to the 130 women who chose to participate. I explained, "On the back, write down what you believe in and what you hope for."

Even though the state count had not yet been cleared, we were permitted to go to the dayroom, to dance with our "worlds" in hand, and to be a part of this global alignment. I put the boom box on a rolling cart and moved the furniture. As we danced, I said, "Y'all, we're gonna rise up and we're going home!" We danced until the count cleared. Then we had to get ready for chow release for dinner. When I look back on that day, miraculously enough, I realize that quite a few of us ladies who danced are home now.

The following day, I collected all our "worlds," put them in envelopes, and mailed them to Carrie in San Diego. She took them to the Capitol in Sacramento and scattered them on the ground in front of the bear statue outside the governor's office, beneath flags we'd probably stretched in prison.

Perkins Coie, the law firm Pat Arthur worked for, had agreed to allow her and five of her colleagues to represent me pro bono. The energy of the Free Sara Kruzan campaign outside the courtroom also continued to gain momentum. My case was receiving a lot of attention because it brought up the issue of sentencing juveniles to LWOP, as well as the growing realization that prostitution is a form of trafficking and so, in effect, slavery.

Shortly before One Billion Rising, on January 18, 2013, Pat and her legal team had reached a deal with the Riverside County Superior Court. In exchange for not appealing their decision, the court reduced the charges against me to second degree murder, which carried a fifteen-year sentence, plus four more years for gun possession. By now I had been incarcerated for nineteen years, including my pretrial year in detention and another at YA before being transferred to Chowchilla. I had already served more than the minimum allotted time under this new sentence. A date was set for my parole hearing on June 12, 2013.

Finding myself in this position seemed nothing short of a miracle, given that I had in effect been told that I would never leave prison unless it was in a pine box. Of course, actually being allowed to go home was far from guaranteed. Because my crime had resulted in a loss of life, I would still need to be assessed by a parole board as to my suitability to rejoin society, and even if the board found me suitable, there was no assurance that the governor would approve their recommendation.

For many who have served their time, appeared before a parole board, and been denied, securing release can feel as elusive as winning the lottery. Some have been denied parole twenty times or more, returning again and again for hearings spread years apart. Historically, those who have committed particularly heinous or sensational crimes have a much lower chance of ever being paroled, even when it is clear that they have been rehabilitated. While the law creates a framework for release, at a parole hearing you are essentially at the mercy of the commissioners deciding your fate. Appointed by the governor, commissioners are frequently retired police officers, former corrections officers, wardens, or prosecutors, whose experience inclines them to suspicion toward those brought before them. More often than not, the justice system is most comfortable taking a punitive approach to rectifying wrongs. During a parole board hearing, the commissioners have the right to grill you about every detail of your life, your crime, and your incarceration.

The possibility of your freedom being granted rides on this exchange, but so many things can derail you. Your nerves may not hold up. The commissioners may not believe that you are taking responsibility for the crime you committed. You may not be articulate enough to express your true thoughts and feelings. Most commonly, the commissioners are unable to accept that you have changed and will deny you parole because of the severity of your crime. Regardless of how long ago you entered the prison system and your accomplishments since that time, the original crime that brought you there is the only way they are able to define you.

Despite all these concerns, during the six months I had to prepare for this momentous appointment to decide my future, I held on to one big, obvious truth for dear life: being eligible for parole, however long it could take, however unlikely it might be, however many times I might have to try, meant that I could wish, dream, and hope that one day I would gain the right to leave prison.

9

On the day of my appearance before the parole board, I woke up feeling happy and confident, though there was no way of knowing what the twists and turns of the hearing would be or whether I'd be successful. In my cell, I listened to "Moment 4 Life" by Nicki Minaj, featuring Drake, to pump myself up so that I could go out and do what I had to do. I changed the lyrics from "This is my moment, I just feel so alive" to "This is my moment to live while doing life." Then I listened to "Hold On, We're Going Home" by Drake and decided I was ready.

My friends walked with me from my cell to the gate leading out to the yard. They gave me lots of hugs and pats on the back as I held up my ducat, allowing me to be escorted to the parole hearing room. As the gate was unlocked by the CO, I could hear my friends: "You got this! Now go, Sara, go!"

Until now, I'd heard of only one person at Chowchilla who found relief in federal court and was able to get an LWOP reversed. People spoke about her release in hushed voices. She was our single beacon of possibility. I took a deep breath to bolster my courage and stepped through the gate, telling myself, "I am going to go in, and I'm going to get a date so that I can get out of here."

When I reached the site of the hearing, I greeted my team

of six lawyers. They all had their game faces on. I now realize that the situation was fraught for them as well. Except for Pat Arthur, who was steeped in the protection of human rights, especially as they pertained to youth, none of the other lawyers had ever appeared before a parole board to support a client. Their firm's specialty was corporate litigation, yet these pro bono litigators had agreed that, in my case, an injustice had been done and I had not received a fair trial. I had been working with the team for years and had developed a close friendship with each of them.

We all knew that how I conducted myself before the parole board would be all that mattered today. They had done their part, fighting for this hearing.

The rooms on the prison grounds where hearings are held are small, which meant that only three of my lawyers, who were in any case there simply for moral support, were permitted to accompany me: Pat and the senior partners Marc Boman and Ron McIntire. Pat and Marc sat behind me, Ron beside me. Next to Ron was a victim's advocate, there on behalf of GG's family. Frequently, family members will also show up and make a victim's impact statement recommending that the perpetrator not be granted parole. In this case, no one did.

A large rectangular table separated us from Walter Johnsen, the deputy commissioner, an older white man, and Ali Zarrinnam, the presiding commissioner, a middle-aged brown man. On a small TV screen was an assistant district attorney from the office of the Riverside DA, Paul Zellerbach, attending via teleconference. The DA's office in the city where your crime took place is allowed to offer commentary during the hearing. A corrections officer from Chowchilla was also present, presumably for protection in case I suddenly lost my mind and became violent. Because Pat and I were the only women present, there was an aura of male dominance in the room.

The proceedings started like a trial: "State your name. Spell your name for the record."

I was gripped by both excitement and fear. On the one hand, I felt strong; I was relieved that this moment was happening. All the same, part of me struggled with a will to elide aspects of my life that I was not proud of. The commissioners had my file in front of them, listing everything: my academic achievements, the books I'd read, the programs I'd completed, the merits I'd earned, but also every 115 I'd received, from talking back to COs to getting into fights. However trivial an incident might seem in retrospect, it could cost you parole. It was tempting to try to justify my rebelliousness, especially when I was first incarcerated, but there seemed little point in doing so given the facts the board was reviewing. On the other hand, who I was and what I had done were not devoid of complexity, and I wanted the commissioners to understand that. Some of my behavior may have seemed irrational, but there were reasons for it. I wanted them to appreciate that I grew up surrounded by people who were violent, scary, and controlling, who held sway over me. As a child who felt helpless, invisible, and unworthy, I had none of that power. Which is not to say that I did not know right from wrong; I simply was not supported or encouraged to make the right choices. I also understood that murdering GG was inexcusable. In brief, I was now thirty-five years old and I had spent a lot of time examining my life. I knew who I was, what had happened, and why.

As I began my prepared remarks, it occurred to me that, except for the video interview with Human Rights Watch, I had never had the chance to speak on my own behalf. I had never had the opportunity to defend myself. During my trial, the judge had denied me and my underpaid and overworked public defender an occasion to properly tell my side of the story. The jury deliberated a shoddily presented case. Here was my moment for redress.

Something seemingly insignificant happened at the start of the proceedings. My microphone had been placed a little too far away from me, and I did not feel comfortable enough to stand up and pull it closer. Zarrinnam noticed that I was leaning and stretching my neck to speak into it, so he got up and pushed the microphone across the table to a better position. To me it was a huge gesture. By making it, Zarrinnam implied that he saw me as a human being deserving of respect, and was invested in what I had to say.

It was a good thing I had decided to tell the unvarnished truth, because the two parole board commissioners I faced that day were there to judge my honesty. The hearing lasted more than four hours; Johnsen and Zarrinnam pounded me with questions to ascertain whether I truly held myself accountable and had sufficient insight into my actions and the choices I had made. They were also there to discover who I was and what I had learned. I was able to admit to and discuss all the circumstances that had brought me there without idealizing myself. So, when Johnsen asked me straight out, "Did you want to kill him?" I answered without hesitation. "There was a part of me that absolutely wanted to kill him. But I did not want him dead, and immediately after I pulled the trigger, I knew that what I'd done was wrong."

I became emotional toward the end of the questioning and noticed that Ron, who was sitting by my side, was emotional too. I felt drained. But as I sat there looking into the faces of the commissioners who would be responsible for deciding if I was suitable to be released, I was pleased that I had had my say. Whether or not I got what I desperately wanted—my freedom—I had told my truth as clearly and fully as I could.

Johnsen and Zarrinnam took a break to deliberate and left the room. When they returned, they announced that they both found me suitable to rejoin society, and that they would file their findings immediately. Within 150 days, I would learn whether the governor upheld their decision. Tears streamed down my face as I listened to the commissioners. Outwardly, I was quiet, smiling through my tears. Inwardly, I was shouting at them, "Thank you thank you thank you!"

It appeared that the Human Rights Watch flyer had proven to be my true golden ducat. My lawyers were as ecstatic as I was. Each had a personal and professional stake in the outcome. In addition to feeling victorious, they were setting precedent, helping to make law, for mine was one of the first cases on record in which "intimate partner battering" had been taken into account as a defense for murder. Yet as high as we were all flying, it was uncertain how the commissioners' decision would be greeted by Jerry Brown, who had replaced Schwarzenegger as governor the previous January. Public pressure regarding my case—all the media attention and lobbying on my behalf—could work in my favor or backfire. The more newsworthy the crime, the greater the risk a governor incurs if he opts for leniency for a prisoner convicted of a violent offense, especially if the governor intends to run for higher office. The specter of Willie Horton looms over every such parole deliberation. Horton was the Massachusetts prisoner who, in 1986, abused a weekend furlough program approved by then governor Michael Dukakis. Horton went on a crime spree, providing George H. W. Bush with ammunition to sink Dukakis's 1988 chances to become president of the United States.

In my heart, I was hopeful that the governor would agree with the commissioners' decision, but when you have experienced the kind of life I have, until you see the proof of something, it's hard to believe it. The justice system had so consistently turned a blind eye to me that I couldn't trust it. We had until mid-November to wait for Brown's decision. As time passed, my anxiety grew. I called my lawyers daily, eager for news, tying myself into a tighter and tighter knot.

October 27, 2013, was a regular Sunday evening after dinner, until it wasn't. I was sitting on an empty white five-gallon bucket, using my bed as a desk, writing to at-risk kids who were students at a San Diego high school. Their teacher, Gabby Baeza, was an advocate for the human rights of youth. She showed her class the Human Rights Watch video in which I appeared, and had her students write to me. She sent me a package of their letters, so that I could write back. Some of the kids asked me about my life or about my incarceration. Some divulged their deepest challenges, secrets, and fears, describing rape, abuse, and situations similar to those I had suffered. These kids felt that they could trust me, and I took my role as mentor to them very seriously.

It was still early. At night, we had close count right before lights-out at 9 p.m. A few of my cellmates were still hanging out in the dayroom watching TV or playing board games. Those of us in the cell were doing our own thing. Lupita, a sweet and warm El Salvadoran, was my best and most trusted friend. Teresa, incarcerated for more than twenty-five years, had been one of my very first bunkies. Stranger was an adorable Mexican woman who looked like Teddy Ruxpin. She was always cracking jokes.

I had my headphones on, grooving, jamming out as I responded to the kids. I was in my own world.

The next thing I knew, Teresa started slamming the bed urgently to get my attention. Her yelling cut through my music: "Sara! Oh my God, girl, you're on TV! You're on TV!"

I jumped up and pulled my headphones down to my shoulders. "What?"

Teresa was pointing at the small television set sitting precariously on a stack of books on her bunk.

"What the fuck?"

We all gathered around to watch, hanging on every word. A news anchor was talking about me. I stood in shock as the *CBS Evening News* flashed pictures from my past. The talking head said that Governor Brown had let it be known that he would uphold the parole board's recommendation for my release. Then my Aunt Anne appeared on screen and started talking about my case, saying, "She'll be paroling to my house."

I started to argue with her. "No, you're wrong." My dad's family had been out of my life during the bulk of the time I'd been in prison, but during the last few years, since the media attention began, they suddenly wanted to be a part of it. Aunt Anne seemed to have decided to be my spokesperson. I was watching incredulously, but I was also thinking, "I'll deal with it later."

Exhaling with relief, I looked around at my friends, suddenly overwhelmed by memories of life with them in the cell. They had all become my sisters. I took in the beautiful faces of Lupita and Teresa, both serving life sentences for murder. I thought about all that we had endured, the fun and the struggles. I would soon be leaving them. It was unlikely that we would ever be together again.

The door was open. I ran down the hall toward the dayroom. Phone #5 was available. I can still hear the sound as I detached the receiver from its cradle on the wall and waited for the dial tone. My fingertips remembered Carrie's phone number even as my brain did not.

I heard the automated message: "You have a call from an

inmate at a correctional facility. . . ." I tapped my foot impatiently and stared out the window, working hard to seem restrained before I finally heard, "Your call has been accepted."

"Hey, Carrie, how are you?" I said as calmly as the situation allowed, wondering if she had heard the news.

"Sara! You're coming home!" Carrie's joy was infectious and affirmed the reality of my parole.

"I just saw it on the news." As I was speaking to Carrie, the Chowchilla grapevine was abuzz with what had been seen and heard on TV. Women streamed from the dayrooms to hug and cheer me on so loudly that I had to hang up. Carrie was laughing as I shouted, "Goodbye!" She understood. I basked in the moment until anxiety from this unfamiliar feeling of excitement and joy began to take over.

I ran back to my cell. Lupita embraced me tightly.

I began to give my things away to my bunkies. All I would be keeping was a clear makeup bag with a few items in it. I handed my letters of support and legal documents to Lupita and told her I would be in touch to let her know my address so that she could mail them later. I told everyone there that I would never forget them and would always be there for them on the outside.

As we sorted through my belongings, Lupita said, "You remember what you promised? You gotta do those cartwheels now."

Years before, I had announced that if I was ever allowed to go home, I would treat the yard to more cartwheels than they had ever seen.

I smiled and said, with conviction, "Hell yeah. I'ma do those cartwheels!"

We played music and danced with abandon before the last count of the night, then tucked ourselves away in our metal bunks for lights-out. I was at once elated and heavyhearted. I was thrilled to be leaving prison and terrified to face a world I no longer knew. I would be leaving behind the only home and family I'd had for nearly twenty years.

On Monday morning I learned that I would be released the following Thursday. Pat Arthur and her legal team had arranged for me, with the state's approval, to be paroled to Orange County under the supervision of Jim Carson, a longstanding advocate for victims of sex trafficking, and my friend. I had known Jim since 2008, when he was working with the Orangewood Foundation, an organization providing support to the youth of Orange County, primarily those in foster care. After seeing my Human Rights Watch video, Jim had written to ask if I would be willing to communicate with a sixteen-year-old survivor who had been through many of the same experiences I had. I immediately agreed. She and I became pen pals and are still in touch today. Jim and I also began corresponding and speaking on the phone regularly. His empathy and understanding of what I had gone through was so evident, I asked if he would visit me. It was a four-hour-plus drive for him, but he began to come to Chowchilla for the weekend, staying at a nearby hotel, and meeting with me during the appointed visiting hours of 9 a.m. to 3 p.m. Saturdays and Sundays.

It took months for Jim and me to develop a bond, and years for me completely to trust him, a middle-aged white man, but sitting at a table talking for six hours at a stretch for five years meant that in time we got to know each other pretty well. Jim cared for me unconditionally. I never felt embarrassed, humiliated, or ashamed when talking to him. One day I asked him if I could call him "Dad." I so badly wanted to have a reliable male figure in my life that I could claim as my own. I was overjoyed when he said, "Of course."

—

Because Jim had for years been so warm, kind, and understanding, I always sought his fatherly advice. From the beginning of my imprisonment, I had received impassioned letters from suitors, perfect strangers, complimenting me on my looks—responding to newspaper or television clips—and offering me romance or marriage. These letters struck me as smarmy and creepy. Incarcerated people, especially those who receive media coverage, are frequently propositioned by mail by bizarrely obsessed men or women. A year or so before I was granted parole, a man (I'll call him Jacob to protect his identity) wrote to me to say that he had seen my video on YouTube and that I reminded him of his sister. She and I looked alike, he said, and our skin was the same shade of brown. He wanted to get to know me and included a photo of himself. Jacob was very attractive and, judging from his letter, polite and well-mannered. He was different from the other letter writers; he seemed genuine, and I believed and trusted what he said. He was an auto mechanic who lived and worked in San Jacinto. After a few letters back and forth between us, he asked for permission to come see me at the prison. I agreed and put him on my list of approved visitors. I invited Jim to chaperone my first "date" with Jacob. Jim was skeptical of my prospective beau and his intentions but agreed to keep an open mind. On the day in question, Jim and I positioned ourselves in the waiting room so that we could look out of the window to see the visitors passing through security at the prison gate.

In person, Jacob looked even more handsome than in his photos, with a fit, muscular physique that he clearly took care to maintain. Jim didn't stay long; as we three chatted, Jim asked Jacob some innocuous questions, then said good-bye and left us to get to know each other. When I called him later for his impressions, Jim told me that he thought Jacob was a good-looking man who seemed harmless enough. I was happy that Jim had, as far as he could, given our relationship his blessing.

Jacob continued to visit me, usually twice a month. He received a lot of attention from the guards. The female staff would make unscheduled appearances and ask me about my gorgeous guest. Jacob enjoyed the attention. Every time he came, he wore a different, fashionable outfit. The peacock in him strutted about the visiting room at Chowchilla, where he knew himself to be somebody. It made him happy and it made me happy, because I had fallen for him. This was all so foreign to me, a man paying me such lavish attention and going out of his way to charm me—a man who wasn't grooming me for trafficking. At some point, the subject of marriage came up and Jacob proposed to me in a casual way. I accepted. I'd always had a fantasy of being loved so much by one man that his love would obliterate all the hurt I had suffered at the hands of others. Jacob would be joining Jim and Carrie to witness and cheer me on my freedom walk.

Because mine was a high-profile case, the prison had been put on alert that there was considerable public interest in my parole. The logistics and timing of my release were shrouded in secrecy in hopes of avoiding a media circus. On Wednesday afternoon at about 4:10 p.m.—twenty minutes before the statewide 4:30 count—I was ordered to report to the office of C yard's lieutenant. As the door was popped open for me, I was handed a ducat—not a white one for something mundane, like a visit to the dentist, but a yellow one, signaling high priority. I was to go to the program office, the headquarters for various educational, religious, and art activities offered at the prison. As I walked there, all was still; everyone was locked down for the count. The lieutenant and the associate warden were waiting for me. Since news of my parole had broken a few days earlier, the prison authorities' paranoia about the media and leaks about where and when my release would happen had centered on family members. The officers gave me a direct order to call my aunt Toni and aunt Anne, my father's sisters, who had volunteered to come get me upon my release.

On speakerphone, I dialed my aunts and informed them that the prison would not allow them to pick me up. When I hung up, I asked for specifics about my last day in prison, and the assistant warden ostentatiously cleared his throat and said that things were still being worked out.

As soon as the count was over, I ran back to my cell block's phone bank to call Carrie to see if she knew what was going on. Only one other person was making a call. After checking the phone list, I scribbled my name on it and waited. I looked down at my faded state-issued blue jeans as I stepped to phone #2 by the window. I wondered if I should take them with me. "Nah," I thought. "They can keep their OG jeans."

Finally, Carrie picked up and accepted my collect call. She was so excited she didn't even say hello. "Sara! I cannot wait for tomorrow!"

I asked her what she knew about my departure.

She said, "Susan and I will be there in the morning!"

"But Carrie," I said. "I don't know what's going on, or what time I am actually being released. They made me call and tell my family not to come."

Just then, I saw Officer McElroy, a too-cute CO with a buff body and tattoos who had always been kind to me. He was heading my way and gesturing conspiratorially.

"Carrie," I said, "hold on. Staff is calling me." I held the phone away from my ear.

McElroy approached and stood very close to me. He spoke in a hushed tone. "Kruzan, you are leaving in the morning right after dark thirty count. Did you know?"

"I didn't. Nobody told me anything."

"All right, don't tell anyone I told you. You cool, and I wanted to let you know 'cause I know you must be worried. And, by the way, I know you gonna do great out there! Congrats! We'll miss you here."

I wondered if I was dreaming as he smiled and swaggered away.

"Carrie, you still there? I just heard they are letting me go after the two-thirty a.m. count. But if they're not letting my family come, I don't know if they'll let you."

On the way back to my room, I passed Ray Ray, a thin blond woman who looked a little like Taylor Swift. We bumped fists and she told me that Lupita had told her about what was happening that evening.

"Be there," I said.

"I will."

Lupita was holding me to my word. She secured permission from the corrections officers to stage a celebration of my freedom in the yard, where we were allowed to hang out after chow from 6:30 p.m. until recall to our cells at 8:45 p.m. She took it upon herself to make posters announcing a gathering that she affixed to walls and light poles on our way to chow that evening. When we returned to our cell, Lupita sat on her bed, which she somehow always managed to keep fluffy and tucked in tightly, tearing scraps of paper for confetti.

I noticed that her head was bent in an unnatural position. It took a few moments for me to realize that tears were spilling from her eyes, leaving mascara tracks streaming down her cheeks. "Hey, girl. Hey, what's up?" I said.

"You know I'm happy for you," she sobbed. "It's just that I'm going to miss you so much."

I hugged her and, of course, began to cry as well. "I'm going to miss you too. Girl, you invited everyone to come and see me do these cartwheels, and look at how you've got me all worked up." I kissed her forehead, pulled away, and went to take my last prison shower.

The warm water cascaded over my head, merging with my tears. I rubbed my body vigorously, furiously, with soap, as if to wash away the last nineteen years in prison, GG's hands on my body, and all the Johns he had arranged to have touch me. Teresa knocked on the shower door, abruptly interrupting my descent into full-on weeping. "Are you ready to do those cartwheels?" she asked. "All the units got Lupita's posters. The yard will be open soon, and your song is playing in the room."

I stepped out of the shower and began to dry off. Back in the cell, Lupita had erased all signs of her tears. She was busy putting the confetti into a big garbage bag.

On the boom box in the cell, Drake was singing, "Just hold on, we're going home . . ." I danced and sang along as I pulled on a pair of gray state-issued sweats and a sweatshirt. Lupita joined in, her wide and graceful El Salvadoran hips swaying to the rhythm of the song. Teresa raised her long arms in the air and began to dance too. Before I knew it, the three of us were shimmying to Drake, and I was dressed and ready to go make an impression and leave in style.

"Let's do this," I said. Lupita was the first to leave the room, carrying her bag of confetti, next was Teresa, and I brought up the rear.

Ray Ray and Alicia, who had cells near mine, lined up behind me as we waited to be let out to the yard. Alicia was a short woman who wore her hair tied up in a bandanna and black-framed glasses. She had such long, curly lashes that they brushed up against the lenses. Alicia really loved singing along to the Meow Mix cat food commercials: "Meow meow meow meow, meow meow meow meow, meow meow meow meow meow meow meow . . ." One day, I caught her in the game room all by herself, singing along to the commercial on TV. "Are you seriously singing the kitty song?" I asked, and never let her live it down.

"Alicia, you gotta sing it for me," I teased her now. "That's your jam. That's your hit song. And I won't be able to hear it after tomorrow. You can't do me like that."

"Yeah, Alicia, sing it," Ray Ray chimed in.

It took a few seconds to get Alicia to sing the kitty song. Her eyes glittered and her cheeks were red with embarrassment, but not the bad kind of embarrassment; she was okay. She sang her heart out for me. Just as she finished, the door buzzed open and I realized that would probably be the last time I'd ever hear her sing.

Lupita rushed out to begin to distribute the confetti. The rest of us clapped for Alicia. I hugged and thanked her. Then we followed Lupita outside.

She had invited the entire community to my performance. As we stepped into the yard, I was stunned by the size of the crowd. A good number of the 256 women in the four units of my section had shown up. High fives, congratulations, and smiles abounded. The weather was mild and inviting. Even Sergeant Schaeffer came to show respect. He was an older white man with a stern bearing. He stood erect in his uniform, as if on military parade. The hint of a smile danced on his lips. Other staff slowly trickled in.

A line of spectators formed to the left and one to the right, leaving a runway-like swath between them. Jordan, a young, athletic, bald Black woman with very white teeth, a beautiful smile, and muscles that made anyone trying to mess with her think twice, came and stood next to me as I stretched and warmed up. She said, "You don't have to do this by yourself. I'll flip with you."

People started whistling and catcalling. "Where them cartwheels at? I don't see no cartwheels. I thought someone said we was gonna see some cartwheels tonight!"

I shut my eyes and said a silent prayer that I should please not embarrass myself. I decided that each cartwheel would represent hope for somebody who had lost their own.

I looked at Jordan and said, "You ready?"

She nodded and called out, "Okay, on your mark, get set, go!"

As Jordan took off, I threw my hands up, focused, and prepared to propel myself down the runway. I felt so strong and confident, for a second I thought I might head into orbit. My hands met damp grass, and I became a spinning wheel, going and going and going, as though my body had a will of its own. The crowd hollered at Jordan and me, cheering us on, counting our revolutions while throwing confetti, contraband glitter, and blades of grass at us. Jordan finished before I did. When I got to the age I was going to turn on my next birthday, thirty-six, I stopped. I was jostled, hugged, and showered with presents: greeting cards, tamales, cookies. I didn't want the jubilation to end, but at 8:45, as happened every night, a voice boomed over the loudspeaker: "Recall." It was time to return to the unit. I left the yard as an "inmate" for the last time that night.

My bunkies and I returned to our cell for the night's lockdown. I knew I wouldn't sleep.

"You have to try," Teresa said.

I couldn't, tossing and turning instead. Before I knew it, the 2:30 a.m. count was done.

A CO unlocked our door and said, "You ready?"

Everyone in the room was still awake. We all hugged. I left the cell, and my friends were locked in for the rest of the night.

As I walked down the hallway, I stopped here and there to say goodbye to people through their cell doors. It seemed as if no one had slept. I left the hallway with sobs echoing in my ears.

It was still dark, and the sky was lit up by the stars I had not seen at this hour for nearly two decades. I followed the CO toward the main building to be processed. Just before leaving, I looked back to catch one last glimpse of the place that had been my home for more than half my life. It looked as though we had just walked a shimmering trail that cut the yard in two. For a moment I felt as if I was in a magical landscape, but then I realized that the yard lights were hitting the confetti and glitter from the evening before. I was happy to be leaving a pathway of hope and possibility behind for the ladies of Chowchilla.

I was driven to R&R (Receiving and Release), where protocols to enter and exit the prison are conducted.

Mrs. Left was the CO on duty handling my release that morning. She was a petite, honey complexioned-colored woman in her late forties with a beautiful smile and a mild-seeming demeanor that could fool you into thinking you could get one over on her. She pointed me toward a large, open cell with peeling paint and handed me some forms to sign along with my parole box, which contained a bright pink tank top, jeans, a pair of high-heeled shoes, and a cozy gray bathrobe, which I wore as a coat because it had turned cold—gifts from a probation officer and a retired social worker with whom I had been friendly in Chowchilla.

I filled out the forms, including a "body receipt" acknowledging that the prison was releasing my body from its possession. I handed them to Mrs. Left, who checked that I had signed in the right places before handing me an envelope containing two hundred dollars: my "gate money." This is what the state of California sends you back out into the world with.

As the staff tried to figure out what to do about the rows of camped-out media sleeping in the prison parking lot. I sat nodding off and daydreaming about meeting up with my friends and Jacob.

"You still here?" asked a female corrections officer arriving to work at 4:30 a.m., jolting me awake. My release was beginning to feel anticlimactic, it was as if I'd thrown a party no one had shown up to. Just after 5 a.m. I was finally whisked into a van with blacked-out windows.

I could hear a commotion outside, but I couldn't see what was happening, which made me feel nervous, so I put on my headphones to tune it out. Finally, at 5:15 a.m. the van left the Chowchilla prison grounds, driving at full speed right past the journalists, as well as Carrie and her entourage, who were waiting there.

Only Jim Carson, who was authorized to pick me up, was notified of where and when to meet me.

I first found myself in a state office building in Bakersfield, where two officers, a man and a woman, put me through more bureaucratic rigamarole. The CDCR still had power over my release, which meant that I had to abide by its rules. The female officer led me into the bathroom for a strip search and drug test. Tired and perplexed, I felt like crying but managed to maintain my composure.

My parole had been set for five years to life, so I needed to register with a parole officer to whom I would report during the coming years, and who would explain to me the regulations that would govern my life from now on. I was driven from one office to another. Several rejected me because of the notoriety of my case and the media attention it continued to attract. Finally, a parole officer in Irvine agreed to have me as his charge. Given the CDCR's paranoia about media coverage, it's ironic that someone at the Irvine parole office took a picture of me that ended up on the news that night. Wearing my bright pink tank top, I looked like a deer in headlights after having had no sleep the night before. Also, apparently for the first time in its history, the CDCR tweeted about a release: mine.

At last, Jim Carson picked me up and took me to my transitional housing in Tustin, a smallish middle-class city in Orange County, where I had been assigned an apartment in a building directly across the street from where he lived. He then drove me to a nearby hotel, where Carrie, Susan, and Jacob were waiting for me. As exhausted as I was, I felt a fresh burst of energy and seized the opportunity to vigorously thank my dear friends—Jim, Carrie, and Susan—who had battled for my freedom for so long.

Carrie and Susan had brought me a large bag of clothes, makeup, and toiletries so that I could hide out without having to navigate shopping just yet. They had thought of everything, even buying me an assortment of bras and underwear from Victoria's Secret. I pulled bikini panties, briefs, thongs, lacy nightgowns, yoga pants, sweats, and more out of a big shopping bag.

Jacob was a little annoyed that I was peeking at my gifts and giggling with the women instead of cuddling him, but after nearly twenty years of wearing the horrible CDCR-approved undies and clothes with absolutely no variety, nothing was going to interfere with this pleasure. The bounty was overwhelming—but so welcome. I finally took off the freedom bathrobe I had worn as a coat to keep warm. In the goody bag was a proper jean jacket. I put that over the pink tank and felt halfway human again. The first and most important thing I wanted to do on my first day of freedom was to visit the ocean.

—

That afternoon, Carrie, Susan, and Jacob drove me to Santa Monica Beach. Running across its expanse, I grabbed a stick and wrote "FREE AT LAST" in big letters in the sand. With Carrie by my side, I entered the waves and submerged myself completely, as if in a baptism.

Suddenly, helicopters appeared overhead, loudly whomping their blades. I panicked, thinking they were coming to get me.

During my final shower at the prison the day before, I had tried to rinse off my last nineteen years and the years before that, but the water from the shower head mingling with my tears had not cleansed me the way I had hoped.

Carrie held me until I was calm. "It's okay," she said. "It's okay."

I emerged from the ocean, feeling shaky but reborn.

10

After moving into my furnished one-bedroom transitional housing apartment in Tustin, I was in shock. Even though I had become the free person I had long aspired to be, I had spent nearly two decades locked away from everyday life and society. The alienation I was experiencing, the waves of shame and sadness, are things I may never shake.

After years of institutional confinement, the day-to-day challenges of life on the outside are many. It was traumatic simply to order from a menu, or to go to sleep and wake up on my own time. Choice is not something you have a right to in prison. Being faced with so many possibilities all of a sudden was overwhelming. I was navigating a world that had changed profoundly. I had to swim, as if from a desert island, into the rough waters of Google, passwords, Word docs, You-Tube, iTunes, IDs, driver's license, credit reports, credit cards.

During those first months of adjustment, Jacob traveled back and forth from my place in Tustin to his auto mechanic job in San Jacinto, about a two-hour drive. He stayed with me when he was in town, which was sometimes less than a week per month. When we were together, he looked into my eyes, and made me feel cared for. He helped me figure out the dishwasher, the internet, and my new cell phone. He went to the mall to buy me fashionable clothes and shoes. I felt hopelessly behind the times with respect to style, technology, and the basic mechanics of daily life, and I deeply appreciated Jacob's help and companionship.

When you leave prison, you are a little paranoid. While there, you learn to watch your back at all times. There are people who will hurt you for no reason. There are hustlers who watch you carefully to spot your weaknesses, the better to exploit you. They might discover a secret and make you pay them to keep it quiet. You learn to keep your business private, so to see my name connected to hits on Google was alarming. I worried that people might come after me. They did—but mostly with good intentions.

Via the Free Sara Kruzan Facebook page, and through Carrie, I was offered speaking engagements, but the idea of addressing a group of strangers about the traumatic experiences I had been through was stressful. I agreed to some. Most memorably, just a few weeks after my release, The Campaign for the Fair Sentencing of Youth honored me with its Healing and Hope Award. Because the terms of my parole did not permit me to appear in person at the ceremony in Washington, DC, I gave my remarks via a live video feed. The organization's mission neatly aligned with my case and with the Human Rights Watch–inspired campaign to free me. Receiving that award so soon after exiting the gates of prison was gloriously exciting. I spoke about Viktor Frankl's book and how it had given me the motivation to stay purposeful and retain a sense of optimism.

People from numerous organizations and all walks of life stepped up to offer friendship and assistance with my reentry into free society. Their generosity was overwhelming, including gifts, monetary and otherwise, that allowed me to buy a car and support myself while I looked for a job. I received a wealth of invitations to participate in various civic initiatives. Luckily, I had Jim, Carrie, and my lawyer, Pat Arthur, to help me sift through the avalanche of correspondence. While I was grateful for so many demonstrations of goodwill, I quickly came to realize that I had to be careful about how I responded, and to whom. While many requests were sincerely intended to be helpful, others sought to harness me and my platform, and the funds at my disposal, to further their own gain.

Pat Arthur explained to me that I had a choice: given the attention I had received, I could seize the interest in me and live in the public eye, or I could opt to guard my privacy. Aware that I needed time to find myself and get to know who I was, freely and peacefully, I chose the latter. I became very selective about how I engaged with the world.

While I was still in prison, Carrie and I had discussed the idea of channeling the support and attention that the Free Sara Kruzan campaign had generated into an ongoing organization in the event of my release. Our mission would be to stand beside, encourage, and support incarcerated women. Besides offering practical guidance, I was eager to provide tools to help them tap into their inner resources and experience hope. I believed that validating incarcerated women's pain and offering a safe place for healing would be a boon, empowering them while they awaited release. Most important, I now had the means to help the women I had left behind in prison.

I was thrilled to be able to make a difference to these women. I knew what they lacked. I put money in their canteen accounts for snacks and toiletries. I sent stationery and stamps to those who did not have families who could fill that need. I sent parole boxes to women who were getting ready to go home. I also began helping some of my friends, who in turn asked me to help their friends, to prepare for parole hearings by counseling them about the process by phone or mail.

I hoped that someday my organization would make a big difference, but that required money, time, and grant-writing and fund-raising skills. Although my good intentions were abundant, I lacked an understanding of how to build a financial portfolio for the organization and myself. It took my running through all that I had been given in order to appreciate that I had a problem that ran deep: Money had bad associations for me. Men had spent money to have sex with me. I had shot and killed a man over money. The more money I was given, the more I felt a need to give it away. Money was a reminder of everything that had led me in the wrong direction, even though I could use it to benefit others, which made me feel good. However, I did not know how to sustain its flow.

My honeymoon phase with Jacob, if you could call it that, was brief. It should come as no surprise that we didn't know each other at all. I am hard-pressed to say whether we even liked each other. He had visited me in prison for eleven months before my successful parole hearing. I had tried to call him every night, but given the intense competition for phone use, the lockdowns, and other obligations and inconveniences of prison life, it was not always possible. Calls are in any case limited to fifteen minutes. Supervised visits held alongside other visitors and fifteen-minute phone calls were not a strong foundation for a marriage.

I was clueless about much of Jacob's life. He admitted to me that when he bought the clothes he had worn to visit me in prison, he had held on to the receipts and kept the tags intact. After each visit, he would return to the department store he favored to exchange one outfit for another to wear the next time. He did not own a car, although he had implied that he did. It turned out he had been renting one for the trips to Chowchilla. I learned that he was deep in tax and credit card debt, which he expected me to help him with.

When he had first brought up the subject of marriage, he told me he was a devout Muslim and that he expected me to adhere to that tradition. I fell in line, agreeing to wear a hijab when we went out. He explained that his religion mandates that no man should see what another man has.

I had no idea what healthy intimacy was. After so many years of living in a single-sex institutional setting, all I knew about heterosexual relationships was what I had seen on TV or read in romance novels, and there the women were usually hyper-focused on making their men happy, so I was poised to make mine happy. When I sent photos of myself at the beach covered from head to toe to friends in prison, they understandably were baffled. My thinking was "I am about to become a married woman, and this is who I am. This is what wives do: follow their husbands' wishes." I was willing to observe the dictates of the Muslim religion without deliberation or understanding. Never mind that while at Santa Monica Beach in a hijab, jeans, and a long-sleeved shirt, I noticed Jacob avidly ogling bikini-clad women as they walked by. His inattentiveness to me now that we were together was painful.

I realize that I could have challenged him, and we might have been able to talk and work things through. I could have said, "You shouldn't impose your beliefs on me without giving me the option to choose," but I didn't because I was afraid of ruining the fantasy I had concocted for myself of getting out of prison and snagging this handsome man who wanted to marry me. After a while, whenever he spent time in Tustin, I would wake up with a sinking, disappointed feeling. I wanted the dream so badly. I would look at him asleep and swallow my growing concerns, while continuing to make marriage plans.

Our wedding, which I paid for, was held at Laguna Beach on Valentine's Day, 2014, three and a half months after my release. Jim refused to have anything to do with the event, so convinced was he by now that Jacob was nothing but a low-level hustler, always crying poverty, claiming that his earnings as an auto mechanic hardly covered his expenses. Jim was also appalled that Jacob was running through my money at an alarming rate.

After the wedding, Jacob and I drove back to my apartment, where I stepped out of my wedding dress and dropped it on the living room couch. I went to the bathroom to take a shower. Jacob was in the kitchen. I wanted desperately for him to come and take me in his arms, hold me, tell me that he loved me, and look at me with the same admiration he had shown when he visited me in prison, but that was not to be. As I closed the bathroom door, I glanced at my ring, which I had purchased myself with money donated to me to help me get back on my feet. Feeling like a fraud, I dried off and got into bed beside Jacob, who was already asleep. I felt as if I had just married myself. We did not hold each other that night. There was no lovemaking. I fell asleep admitting to myself that I had made a big mistake.

The next morning, Jacob went back to San Jacinto. He was gone for a couple of weeks. We spoke on the phone now and then without saying much. We were not physically intimate again until two weeks later, at the end of February, when he returned to Tustin.

About three weeks after that, when I began to cry inexplicably at odd moments, Jacob was the first to say, "I think you're pregnant." I bought a pregnancy test. I went into the bathroom and tested myself twice to confirm the first positive result. I pondered the state of my marriage. "It's going to be fine," I reasoned. "You can handle this." I left the bathroom and went over to Jacob, who barely looked up from his phone, and said, "I'm pregnant."

"I hope it's a boy. It's an honor to have a boy first."

"If it's a girl, that's great too," I responded, and walked away.

I told myself, "Sara, now you've gone and done it. You're stuck." I did not want to bring a baby into the world without a father. Defeated, I sat on the couch. I took inventory of my life—the cooking, the cleaning, the paying for Jacob's rental cars (and giving him money for whatever he needed). The picture was not pretty: Jacob contributed nothing to the marriage.

When the sonogram technician told me I was having a girl, and that she had never seen a baby curled up in such a tight fetal position, I knew something had to give. "I am blessed to be your mother, little girl," I whispered. I decided I would no longer endure the status quo with Jacob. I texted Jim and told him everything, and he helped me chart a course of action to escape from the marriage.

My ambivalence about money showed itself yet again: In separating from Jacob, I wanted to share some resources with him. Initially, I debated giving him my car, but I figured I would need that, so Jim and I went to the bank. I withdrew five thousand dollars in cash and put it in a bag. Jim took me to a nearby hotel, where I hid out while he went off to confront Jacob. He told Jacob to pack up his things, gave him the money, collected his keys, and dropped him off at another hotel. Jacob took the money and left town without giving me any more trouble, and that was that. Six months after my release from prison I was expecting a child, and my marriage was over.

—

In retrospect, I am sure that, as unhappy as I was with Jacob, he was also unhappy with me. Neither of us knew what we were getting into. I was heartbroken that the marriage had not worked, but as soon as he left, I felt immediate relief. I knew I had done the right thing.

After Jacob was out of my life, I tried to take it easy and look after myself in my pregnancy. I had started figuring out how to use Facebook and was having fun finding and getting in touch with old friends. One day, to my surprise, I came across a woman named Dolores Canales. I remembered her. We had been in the honor dorm together at Chowchilla. She was a small woman, standing about five foot one, with dark brown hair, a radiant smile, and a happy, boisterous laugh. Everyone called her Nana because she was like the ultimate grandma, always willing to feed you and help you. No matter the problem, Nana would be there for you. She is now the community outreach director for The Bail Project, a national organization whose mission is to combat economic inequality in the cash bail system.

At Chowchilla, we were friendly but not close. She had been released four years before me, in 2009, but when I reached out to her, she answered me right back. I told her I was pregnant and mentioned that I had a checkup the next day. She asked me who was going to the appointment with me, and I said I was fine going alone. Dolores insisted on accompanying me.

I had bled a few times during the first trimester and been sent home from the emergency room with orders to rest. I was now in my sixth month. At my checkup that day, the doctor gave me a Doppler ultrasound, then left the room with a worried face to seek a second opinion. His colleague came in, examined me, and said, "I'm sorry, but we have to admit you. This pregnancy is high risk."

I looked into Nana's worried eyes and said, "It's going to

be okay. I feel it." But I was scared too. I held on to her hand tightly. We had to drive to UC Irvine for me to be hospitalized. In Radiology I'm sure the technician sensed my fear, though I was trying desperately to be calm. She squeezed the cold gel on my stomach and stared hard at the screen. I closed my eyes and prayed that my child was still alive.

"Mamacita," the technician said. "This baby is blessed. She has a strong heartbeat." Relief flooded over me. I was taken to a room and placed on full bed rest. The goal was to get me to thirty-four weeks. Nana insisted on moving into the hospital with me so I wouldn't be alone. They set up a little cot beside my bed for her to sleep in.

At first, the doctors thought I had toxoplasmosis, a parasitic infection, but they ruled that out, having realized that the complication was with the placenta and the umbilical cord. The baby was not growing properly; she was underweight and barely moving. They diagnosed me with placental insufficiency and intermittent diastolic blood flow, a mysterious condition that can be tied to drug use, but I was clean. They were worried that my daughter might be born blind or without fully developed limbs. The doctors kept informing me that, because I was already in my seventh month, I could not abort the baby. I did not want to. I told them, "God gave me this baby. If she is meant to be born, she will be, and I will love her."

I experienced several terrifying incidents when the fetus was in distress and the monitoring alarms went off. The emergency technicians would run into my room ready to rush me off for a C-section if needed. They would have me sit up and move because the baby's heart rate had dropped. Once it fell dangerously low. I jumped out of the bed and said, "No, you can't quit. Please don't quit! Come on, girl." Her heartbeat resumed with fuller force. "This baby's going to live," I said to the wide-eyed nurses staring at me.

During the day, when Nana left to run errands or do some work, Jim or my sister, Mya, would come by. Sometimes I would drift off to sleep and wake to find Jim, Mya, Nana, doctors, and nurses all camped out in my room. The doctors would say, "Go back to sleep. We like sitting in here because it's so peaceful." For a month I listened to my baby's heartbeat on the monitor. Apart from those frightening moments when it dropped, for thirty days straight her little heart beat a loud, insistent rhythm in my room. My due date was December 14, but on September 30 at 10:19 a.m., I was given an epidural and wheeled to the operating room for a C-section. I counted about twelve people there—the emergency NICU team, the obstetrics team, the anesthesiologist, Nana. We were all waiting for my daughter to be born.

I had gained about sixty pounds during the pregnancy, so I thought she was going to be a good-sized baby. I was shocked that she weighed only two pounds. She did not cry. They whisked her into an incubator and out of the room before I could see her. A few hours later, the nurse came in to give me pain medication and told me my newborn had stabilized. "I need to see my baby," I told her. She wheeled me to the NICU, and when I laid eyes on her, I knew true love for the very first time.

I named her Summer Reign-Justice Kruzan. Her name makes me think of a song by Carl Thomas and feel as if my favorite season and the warmth of the sun will rule over my life forever. Summer was tiny but fine. Her organs were all functional. She didn't need oxygen. Her lungs were fully formed. She was not blind. Her heartbeat was strong. She had ten fingers and ten toes. The first time they rolled her bassinet into my room, I played the Pharrell Williams song "Happy," and that tiny baby began to move her arms and fists, as if dancing. Nana and I cried and laughed. We both knew for sure that Summer was a force to be reckoned with. On October 31, we were allowed to leave the hospital. Summer was just a few ounces under four pounds, but she was healthy and deemed suitable for discharge. I had been released from prison exactly one year earlier, to the day. I think about that coincidence a lot.

Being a mother has at times threatened to overwhelm me, but I have never allowed that to happen. Providing for my child—clean sheets, clothes, balanced meals, toys, books—requires concentration and effort. I was emotionally underdeveloped after spending so many years cut off from normal interactions. I don't always know what motherhood looks like, but I do know that I don't ever want my child to feel the way I did. GG was able to lure me into a nightmare simply by offering me ice cream; I make sure I always have plenty of ice cream at home. When telling my story, I sometimes try to explain my mother's parenting of me in terms of a glass of water: Her water was dirty. She didn't have clean water to give me. It is my duty now to make sure the water I give Summer is always clean.

I had wanted to provide a stable two-parent home for my child, but the universe redefined my notion of what a loving home and family ought to be. To my great good fortune, my community of formerly incarcerated women rallied around me to offer their support in raising Summer: babysitting, sharing their own children's clothes, providing diapers and toys and, best of all, friendship. Their involvement has made my satisfaction at bringing a child into the world more complete than I could ever have imagined.

I didn't see my mother again until three years after I had left prison. My sister, Mya, Summer, and I drove six hours to Oregon, where Mom had moved not long after my sentence began. Her new home looked a lot like the house in Rubidoux. She still had cats and still collected "antiques." I hadn't seen her since before I was incarcerated at Chowchilla, and hoped that now, more than twenty years later, things would magically be okay between us. But it was immediately clear that Mom hadn't changed. She complained. She blamed. She felt sorry for herself. Being around her was nothing but stress. Still, for a few hours that day in Oregon, we were all polite to one another. Mom was warm toward Summer and hugged her and told her she loved her. At one point, we went outside, just the two of us. We sat in silence for a while. Then she began to laugh and told me she was sorry. She didn't elaborate on what she was sorry about, and I still don't know why she was laughing. I didn't press her; that would have been pointless. She is who she is. I've forgiven her in my heart, but I speak with her only very rarely by phone. I, along with my brother and sister, refuse to have much to do with her.

Summer is still small. She just turned seven, and on a good day, she weighs forty-five pounds. At her last physical exam, she stood three feet, five inches, but the doctors say she is fine—in my opinion, she is better than fine. My Summer is tiny in body but mighty in spirit. Her personality is radiant; she lights up any room she enters. For someone so young and petite, she has a deep voice, a quick wit, and a hearty laugh. She's intelligent and athletically fearless. From the moment Summer was born, I decided that everything I did would be for her and to honor her.

11

When I was still a few years away from being released from prison, I received a letter from a lawyer named James Dold. He served as the senior policy counsel for the Polaris Project, an NGO working for the abolition of human trafficking, and had been asked to advise the organization on whether it should join the Human Rights Watch campaign for clemency for Sara Kruzan. James researched my case, read my trial transcripts, and was outraged by what he discovered. In addition to offending his sense of justice, my circumstances resonated with him on a personal level: As a child, he had himself been preyed upon, and all his life he had shouldered the burden of that experience. In fighting for the rights of people like me, he would also be fighting the wrongs he had suffered as a boy. James strongly recommended that Polaris support my application for clemency.

In my post-Chowchilla life, I dedicated myself to unearthing and tracking facts and fictions about sex trafficking. Like James and others who provided me with support and inspiration, I wanted to promote a better understanding of how to tackle the issues within our justice system, and to help lift up others like me who had been victims of both trafficking and disproportionate sentencing as a result of crimes against our abusers. Sex trafficking is commonly defined as "the use of force or fraud to coerce another person to provide sex for money." Of the more than 23,500 runaways reported to the National Center for Missing and Exploited Children in 2018, at least one in seven were likely to be victims of child sex trafficking. Though its prevalence—not just in far-flung parts of the world but here at home—is often overlooked, the trafficking of children is an abuse that leads to a multiplicity of traumas, both physical and psychological. Vaginal and anal tearing, pain, infection, unwanted pregnancy, HIV, syphilis, herpes, hepatitis B and C, depression, PTSD, tuberculosis, sexual and personality confusion, and addiction can all be part of the picture.

The Polaris Project debunks the stereotypical myth that a stranger in a windowless van kidnaps children and rents them out on the street for sex. Kidnapping is rare; trafficked individuals generally already know their traffickers. Recruitment and grooming are the ways traffickers win the trust of their targets, and they usually prey on abused children living in unstable settings by luring them with treats and gifts, the way GG lured me.

One of the most common misconceptions about the sex trade that distorts the public's understanding of it is the notion that trafficked persons have agency and can exercise choice in the matter. Children are not able to make informed decisions about sexual consent, nor should they be expected to, and they are usually hard pressed to escape the predations of adults. I believe that the most important requirement for preventing the sexual exploitation of children and other victims of trafficking is empathy, and I was ready to lend my voice to the effort to inspire empathy in others.

When I first met James Dold in person in November 2014, a year after my release, I had no idea how important he would later become to me, my life, and my legacy. He had invited me to Washington, DC, on behalf of the Campaign for the Fair Sentencing of Youth (CFSY) to attend a roundtable discussion about abolishing Juvenile Life Without Parole (JLWOP) nationwide by getting a bill signed into law. At the meeting, I watched in awe as James explained the legislative process. He was animated, thorough, and articulate as he described the nine steps between a bill's drafting and its approval. That's without taking into consideration roadblocks, detours, reviews, revisions, a possible veto, and the overruling of that veto. All of this takes time. Before a bill can be voted on by the House of Representatives and the Senate, years, even decades, might go by, but once a state agrees to support a bill, things can snowball from there.

After the presentation, in a private chat with me, James elaborated on the abuse he himself had endured. More so than most advocates for change I had met, James, a young man of mixed race, looked at me, saw me, and empathized with me in a way that really touched me because of our similar experience. I offered to help advance his mission in whatever way I could, and he invited me to join him and others on a trip to Henderson, Nevada, to meet with legislators in the spring of 2015. There we would speak about why JLWOP and other harsh sentences given to minors were so unjust. We would serve as examples of the sorts of people the system attempts to lock away for the rest of their lives.

At the Henderson courthouse, James addressed the legislative committee that had convened to hear his arguments. He outlined the history of extreme sentencing and stressed the importance of giving judges the power to consider mitigating factors such as the age and the legal responsibility of children when determining their culpability. He described the ways in which children are fundamentally different from adult defendants. He highlighted factors that are too often ignored by courts, such as coercion by an adult, a history of abuse or trauma, or the child's actual role in the offense. He included the fact that the juvenile crime wave of the 1980s and the "superpredator" theory popularized in the 1990s by the political scientist John Dilulio Jr., then a professor at Princeton, had helped to usher in harsher crime laws and the prosecution of children as adults.

James introduced the three of us who had come to share our personal stories with the legislators. First was Xavier McElrath-Bey, a formerly incarcerated man who now works as a youth justice advocate. When he was just thirteen years old, Xavier was sentenced to twenty-five years in prison for gang-related first-degree murder. While serving his sentence, he earned two associate's degrees and a bachelor's degree. Next was Mario Taylor, who had received a ninety-year sentence at the age of fifteen for first-degree murder. While incarcerated, he had earned his GED and mentored incarcerated youth, continuing to offer support to young people after his sentence was commuted by Nevada governor Kenny Guinn and he was released from prison. Mario showed that, despite his past, he could make a positive contribution to society.

Then I addressed the committee and talked about the fact that I had received an LWOP sentence for a murder I committed at age sixteen. I described my experience of being trafficked, manipulated in GG's robbery and murder, and punished for all of it. I said that I wanted to put a human face on the kids whose lives we were talking about. I explained that at one point I had a 4.0 GPA and that I was raised by a single mother who was addicted to drugs and who abused me. This, I insisted, did not excuse my crime. I carried it with me every day, but it wasn't all that I was. I spoke about being tried as an adult, unable to understand the legal jargon that sealed my fate, and having been denied the opportunity to account for my life and crime as I understood them. I closed by saying that I knew there were many incarcerated young people who, if given the possibility to redeem themselves, would prove that they were worthy of a second chance.

My testimony was met with shock and disbelief. One of the lawmakers remarked that I should have received a medal, not a prison sentence.

In 2015, Assembly Bill #267 passed unanimously through both houses of the Nevada legislature, making Nevada the thirteenth state to abolish a sentence of life without the possibility of parole for juvenile offenders.

After the trip, I remained in touch with James Dold, whose campaign to end LWOP sentences for youth under any circumstances continued to build momentum and support. One day he called with an idea that floored me. "I know a way to change your narrative to something positive," he said. "You have been wronged by so many entities: your family, GG, and the justice system. You should receive reparations of some sort. Unfortunately, we can't arrange anything like that. But here's what we can do: We can put pen to paper and create a law to change the outcomes for children like yourself. Because of this law, no child will suffer what you did, and we're going to name it Sara's Law, after you."

I was not sure that a law should be named after me, but James felt that my case and the campaign to free me was one of the sparks that had ignited the movement to end JLWOP. James suggested that Sara's Law could be considered a form of public apology and recognition that what had happened to me, and others like me, was wrong. When he put it that way, I agreed.

James, who authored the bill, defines it this way: "Sara's Law-HB 3135 is a law designed to protect child sex abuse, rape, and sex-trafficking victims who commit acts of violence or other crimes against the people who abused, raped, or exploited them. It authorizes judges to depart from any mandatory sentence, suspend any sentence, and transfer the child victim back to juvenile or family court for proper adjudication and treatment services there."

Virginia has been the first state to adopt Sara's Law, but in a slightly different form. Virginia House Delegate Vivian Watts shepherded bill #HB744, which requires judges to consider a minor's exposure to adverse childhood experiences (ACE) and any prior involvement in the child welfare system before rendering a sentence. In an article that appeared in *The Virginian-Pilot* in May 2020, Delegate Watts wrote that three cases that make laws like this imperative are mine and those of two other trafficking victims, Cyntoia Brown and Alexis Martin.

The Oklahoma House Judiciary took the first big step toward the approval of Sara's Law in a 14-1 vote in 2020. And despite the delays caused by Covid-19, the bill continues to be presented to a growing number of state legislatures for review.

Three years after my release, I was offered a position working with the Los Angeles–based organization Healing Dialogue and Action (HDA), which practices the principles of restorative justice within both the free and incarcerated populations. Under its auspices, I held group meetings at juvenile halls with recently arrested youth, using the strategies I'd learned in the Alternatives to Violence training.

A few months into the job, an opportunity came up for me to go back to Chowchilla to conduct a seminar and information session highlighting restorative justice principles. I woke early to drive the five hours down the freeway to get there.

I sat for a moment in my car in the parking lot to compose myself. Before reentering the prison where I had spent so many years, I reminded myself that this time I could leave at will. I walked into Chowchilla with no chains around my waist, and no shackles on my ankles. "I'm not an 'inmate' anymore." For a second, I felt woozy and almost lost my balance, but I took a deep breath and told myself, "You said you would be back, and you are. Get it together."

I handed my ID to the watch commander before being let through the heavily guarded gates and locked doors,

The CO checking my ID recognized me and gave me a nod and a smile as he handed me the visitor's badge to clip to my blouse. I attached it carefully, understanding that it signaled to everyone that I was free to walk out of there.

As I passed through the control center and headed to the trailer in the yard where groups are held, I stopped for a moment to admire the white and pink roses. They were one of the things that used to bring me joy at Chowchilla whenever I saw them. The flower beds were an oasis en route to the desert-like dirt and concrete of the yard and the barbed-wire and electric fences beyond it. "Sara!" someone shouted, interrupting my nature break. I looked over and saw a crowd of women waiting for the class dressed in the drab clothes I used to wear. They were jumping up and down with excitement to see me, and ran up to greet me. "Girl, look at your shoes!" someone said, pointing at my pumps with flower appliqués.

The tears shot from my eyes like twin waterfalls. The ladies were also crying. We all knew that only handshakes are allowed between a volunteer and an "inmate"—because of this, in prison, shaking hands with a free person has special meaning— yet we broke the rules that morning. In our big group hug, I couldn't distinguish one woman from the next. My escort, a young white CO I vaguely recognized, sighed and turned her head as if to say, "I'm going to pretend I'm not seeing this, but hurry up." I finally pulled myself away and dried my tears, and, sounding as professional as possible, said, "Let's go into the trailer." I realized that if a less compassionate CO happened to pass by, my friends' hugging me could cost them a 115, and I would be banned from ever coming there again.

About thirty women attended the workshop. We sat in a circle and gave our names. When I said mine, the group cheered. After the initial elation of reunion, we got down to business and held a productive session about taking responsibility for ourselves and the consequences of our actions. There were a lot of raised hands. The question that kept coming up was "What is it like to be free?"

I had no good answer. Every person's experience is completely different. We all make mistakes, but every new day of freedom is a victory. I couldn't tell them that I still woke every morning at five-thirty no matter how late I fell asleep. Or that choosing the clothes I wear each day or what food I should buy from the supermarket is taxing after having had no option besides what the system has chosen for you. I didn't want to dampen anyone's hope and joy by explaining that it is a struggle to make ends meet and not to let the stress overwhelm you. But I also didn't want to taunt them with the fact that I could stand outside at night, breathe in the air, and look at the stars, or drive to the beach whenever I felt like it and let the wet sand scrunch between my toes and warm waves lap over my feet. I told them they would all get there because if I could do it, they could too. I vowed to be there for them when they walked through the gates into the sunshine of freedom. And I meant it.

Saying good-bye that first time was difficult. I've been back to Chowchilla, as well as to other facilities, to lead workshops. It gets easier each time I walk into a prison, knowing that I can walk out again. But it's never easy to leave behind those you love, and those you have come to know.

As I returned to my car that first day, I knew that for those women to have seen me was proof that it was possible to find a way out of no way out. And for me, it was a magnificent example of understanding what survival is. It is facing something, looking it in the eye, and saying, "Now what?"

Restorative justice is not an infallible route to forgiveness, but it is the best method we have to come to terms with harm we have caused and suffered. In my shakier moments, I am forced to recognize the fact that I cannot go back and change the trajectory of my life. The heartbreak still creeps up on me from time to time as I continue to confront the moments that brought me to the Dynasty Suites on March 10, 1994. I may never be done trying to face them.

Coda

One November day, when Summer was old enough for me to feel comfortable leaving her with a babysitter, I set out to meet Roosevelt, who had abused me when I was a child and who I had not seen for more than twenty years. As a new mother to a daughter whom I wanted to protect from ever experiencing what I had gone through, I felt driven to confront him. I found him on Facebook and worked up the nerve to contact him and ask him if he'd be willing to meet. He was open to it. I didn't know much about his life except that he was working as a building superintendent.

We met on a bright, sunny Saturday at Fairmount Park in Riverside, California, at two in the afternoon. The place I chose for the meeting was significant: It was the same park that he would take me to when he was "mentoring" me. It is also close to Locust Street, where the car accident that killed my best friend Shawna Lee had taken place, which gave me the opportunity to drive down the street beforehand and hold her in my thoughts.

As I drew closer to Fairmount Park, I began to feel a tug of worry. My phone pinged a text message from Roosevelt while I was parking. Was he backing out? No. He had written, "I'm here by the pond, on a bench, wearing a white T-shirt."

"Okay," I thought, as I got out of the car, "here we go."

Hesitantly, I walked toward the bench where he was waiting. I was genuinely grateful that he was willing to show up. Here, at last, was my moment to ask him for answers to questions I had spent so long asking myself. For nearly twenty years in prison, I had reflected on the insecurity and confusion caused by his actions and had agonized over them.

Memories of his assaults flooded my mind as I approached the pond. I began to question my decision to come there, but willed myself to keep walking. And then I was standing in front of him. He stood up from the bench—he was so much shorter and less powerful than I remembered. His hair was graying, as was his beard.

We shook hands as though we were meeting for the first time, and sat down next to each other. The moment was at once familiar and strange. My heart was thumping. I took a deep breath to attempt to steady myself. "Thank you, Roosevelt, for meeting me," I said. As I spoke, I felt my pulse begin to slow down to a reasonable pace.

Roosevelt didn't look at me directly. He was scanning the trees and his mind seemed far away. For a while, we sat quietly, both lost in our separate thoughts. I reflected to myself, "How courageous of him to show up after all these years."

Eventually, he broke the silence: "How have you been?" His eyes were focused on the ground. His hands remained folded in his lap.

I began to share with him what I had been up to since my release from prison. I was animated, talking a mile a minute about the weather, my health, Summer, everything I could think of.

He listened quietly. He looked everywhere but at me. I was not offended by his lack of eye contact. It seemed respectful. After I had chattered some more, we again sat in silence. Suddenly the air felt heavy. It was time. I gathered up my courage and calmly said, "Would you please look at me, Roosevelt?"

He did, and I saw profound sadness in his eyes.

"I believe that what I'm going to say, and what I'm asking of you, is going to be difficult for the two of us. But my soul needs to be heard and acknowledged by you, and I'm here to ask you . . . I'm here to ask you, Roosevelt, why?"

His eyes watered; he closed them and sighed, as if in defeat.

I said, "This is a safe space for us to share. I am not here to judge you. I just want to know why you did those things to me. I was a child. I didn't understand. I need to know so that I can heal and try to become myself again."

He shook his head. Tears dropped from his eyes. He quickly wiped them away. "I know, I know," he whispered.

I took a deep breath and continued. "How could you force sex on a twelve-year-old child? So much sex. Why did you think it was okay to ejaculate all over my face in this park so many times? Why did you take me to motels when I was supposed to be in school? How could you, a grown man, have this type of interaction with me, a child?"

He dropped his head into his hands and wept.

"I'm not here to cause harm. I don't want to hurt you." I said. "Are you all right?"

He nodded yes, and in a barely audible tone said, "It's okay. I know I need to hear this."

He continued to cry. Each tear that fell from his eyes felt like an expression of his remorse and a plea for forgiveness. I put my arm around his shoulders to console him. Tears welled up in my eyes, too. Together we grieved.

Time seemed to stand still. "What a gorgeous day," I thought. There were no clouds in the deep blue sky. I inhaled the musky smell of the pond and the perfume of the flowers planted around us in the park.

Finally, Roosevelt lifted his head, looked at me, and began to speak. He unburdened himself; it was my time to listen. He too had been a victim of traumatic abuse as a child, and of gang violence. He explained that, to him, when he was growing up, it was normal to objectify girls and women. It never crossed his mind that I was just a child.

Somehow I understood. In my own life, there had always been a thin line between child and adult.

Roosevelt said, "I am a father and a grandfather now. And I would never want what I did to you to be done to anyone in my family. I'm so sorry, Sara."

"Thank you for saying that. Thank you," I said.

I closed my eyes and covered my heart with my hands. As I accepted his apology, I could feel my face breaking into a gentle smile. When I opened my eyes, I saw that Roosevelt was mirroring me. He had closed his eyes and there was a gentle smile on his face.

We said goodbye, hugged, and walked away.

Acknowledgments

Please know that even if your name isn't mentioned you are still in my heart and soul, and without you this wouldn't be a reality:

Adisa, Aimee Itchikawa, Alicia "Kitty," my sister Mya, Angelyn Frazier, Anna Anthony, Amy and Clay and family, Pat, Bethany, Mr. Butler, Carissa Phelps, Carrie, Susan, Cheryl Face, Christina D., Classy and Liberty, Clinton H., Cori Thomas, Dana, Dana Bryan, Demetria, Dolores aka Nana, Don Knabe and family, Donita F., Earlonne, Elizabeth Calvin, Earthsay Love, Eve MacSweeney, Erroll McDonald, Gina, Gweenie, Hanniah, Harriet H., Irene Hu, Judy and my love for Shawna forever, Julie, Keith and the crew at Uncommon Law, LaShunda, Lupita, James Dold, Jim Carson, Jody, Joy A., Judy Conner, Kathy and Jeff, Kirn Kim, Krissy K., Lois Starr, Michelle and Patty, Mitzi, Najwa, Pearl Graves, Roberta and Jim McLaughlin, Robin Levinson, Sandy Jones, Sistah Soul and Michael, Sybil Grant, Tabatha, Lt. Cooper, Ray;

My Perkins Coie Team: Marc Boman, Michael Teter, Kelly Moser, Pat Arthur, Ron McIntire, Melora Garrison, Allison Parker;

Commissioners Johnsen and Zarrinnam, Governor Arnold Schwarzenegger.

Special thanks to everyone who supported the campaign to free me from prison.

May we continue to heal together.

With deep gratitude,

Simply Sara

I would like to thank:

Sara Kruzan for entrusting me with your story,

My brilliant agent Eve MacSweeney, who goes above and beyond,

Ian Manuel, Nancee Bright, Carrie Christie, James Dold, Dolores Canales, Jim Carson, Michelle Guyman, Patti Dixon, Timothy Brown, Mike Kurth, Connie Nunez, Earlonne Woods, Pearl Graves, Malcolm Butler, Judith Ann Jennings, Liff and Carey Thomas, Jane Rosenthal, Bella Hatkoff, Lourdes Thomas Leahy, Blonnie Thomas, Natasha and Matt Diaz, Joan Hornig, Jessica Dickey and Benoit Bardy, David Jassy, Lonnie Morris, Kirsten Jacobson, Vern Co, Leah Hamos, Emery Bright, Berry Welsh, Marlice Rocha, Nigel Poor, Lauren Sandler, Dr. Kimberly Van Zee, Dr. Peter Cordeiro, Cindy Cooper, Kia Corthron, Cherie McNaulty,

Sara's legal team at Perkins Coie with special thanks to Melora Garrison and Ron McIntire.

Lisa Lucas, Erroll McDonald and the team at Pantheon, including: Vanessa Haughton, Victoria Pearson, Josefine Kals, and Yuki Hirose.

From the bottom of my heart,

Cori Thomas

A NOTE ABOUT THE AUTHORS

Sara Kruzan, a survivor of sex trafficking, is an advocate for the rights of incarcerated women and children. She and her daughter, Summer, live in California.

Cori Thomas is an author, a screenwriter, and an award-winning playwright. She lives in New York City.

A NOTE ON THE TYPE

This book was set in a version of the well-known Monotype face Bembo. This letter was cut for the celebrated Venetian printer Aldus Manutius by Francesco Griffo, and first used in Pietro Cardinal Bembo's *De Aetna* of 1495.

Typeset by Scribe,
Philadelphia, Pennsylvania

Printed and bound by Sheridan Minnesota,
a CJK Group Company, Brainerd, Minnesota

Design by Michael Collica